2nd Workshop on Deriving Insights From User-Generated Text (WIT 2022)

Dublin, Ireland
27 May 2022

ISBN: 978-1-7138-6755-5

Printed from e-media with permission by:

Curran Associates, Inc.
57 Morehouse Lane
Red Hook, NY 12571

Some format issues inherent in the e-media version may also appear in this print version.

Printed with permission by Curran Associates, Inc. (2023)

Association for Computational Linguistics
209 N. Eighth Street
Stroudsburg, Pennsylvania 18360

Phone: 1-570-476-8006
Fax: 1-570-476-0860

acl@aclweb.org

Additional copies of this publication are available from:

Curran Associates, Inc.
57 Morehouse Lane
Red Hook, NY 12571 USA
Phone: 845-758-0400
Fax: 845-758-2633
Email: curran@proceedings.com
Web: www.proceedings.com

WIT 2022

2nd WIT - Workshop On Deriving Insights From User-Generated Text

Proceedings of the Workshop

May 27, 2022

The WIT organizers gratefully acknowledge the support from the following sponsors.

Megagon Labs

Introduction

Welcome to the 2nd WIT (Workshop On Deriving Insights From User-Generated Text)!
Recent advances in Conversational AI, Natural Language Processing, Natural Language Understanding, Language Generation, Machine Learning, Deep Learning, Knowledge Bases, and others, have demonstrated promising results and far-reaching uses of text. Such results can be seen in many different tasks including, but not limited to better extractions from user-generated content, better language models, new approaches related to (commonsense) knowledge-bases, knowledge graphs, better information seeking QA (or Dialogue) systems, etc. Classical data management problems such as data cleaning/integration and search may also benefit from these new approaches.
The WIT workshop series was started to provide a venue to exploit and explore the use of advanced AI/ML/NLP techniques on user-generated text, which is rich in user insights and experiences. Therefore, the goal of this workshop series is to bring together researchers interested in the development and the application of novel approaches/models/systems to address challenges around harnessing text-heavy user-generated data that is available to organizations and over the Web.
For this 2nd edition, the workshop will have a great line-up of invited speakers (Mirella Lapata - University of Edinburgh, Rada Mihalcea - University of Michigan, Ann Arbor, Nina Balcan - Carnegie Mellon University, Carlos Guestrin - Stanford University) as well oral (and poster) presentations of contributed research papers. Following the tradition started in the 1st WIT, the 2nd WIT will host a panel of experts from the academia and industry to discuss and share their experiences and challenges faced in deriving insights from user-generated text. The panel is tentatively titled "User generated content and deep learning: Sorting out 'the good, the bad, and the ugly"' and is intended to highlight and surface the effects of training data on downstream applications and whether or not organizations prepare efforts around removing biases in data that they use for training or other purposes.
We would like to congratulate the authors of accepted papers, as well as to thank all the authors of submitted papers, members of the Program Committee and all the ACL main conference organization team.
2nd WIT Organizing Committee

Organizing Committee

General Chairs and Program Chairs

Estevam Hruschka, Megagon Labs Inc.
Tom Mitchell, Carnegie Mellon University
Dunja Mladenic, Jozef Stefan Institute
Marko Grobelnik, Jozef Stefan Institute
Nikita Bhutani, Megagon Labs Inc.

Program Committee

Program Committee

Sara Abdali, Georgia Institute of Technology
Shabnam Behzad, Georgetown University
Arthur Brazinskas, University of Edinburgh
Brett Zhiyuan Chen, Google
Maisa Duarte, Bradesco Bank – Brazil
Nelson Ebecken, COPPE/UFRJ Federal University of Rio de Janeiro – Brazil
Jacob Eisenstein, Google
Joao Gama, University of Porto – Portugal
Tianyu Jiang, University of Utah
Hannah Kim, Megagon Labs
Aljaz Kosmerlj, Viaduct.ai
Thom Lake, Indeed.com
Yutong Li, Apple
Jun Ma, Amazon
Vagelis Papalexakis, UC Riverside
Jing Qian, University of California Santa Barbara
Sajjadur Rahman, Megagon Labs
Yutong Shao, UC San Diego
Evan Shie, Amazon
Nedelina Teneva, Amazon
Xiaolan Wang, Megagon Labs
Xinyi (Cindy) Wang, Carnegie Mellon University
Yusuke Watanabe, Amazon
Chris Welty, Google
Natasha Zhang Foutz, University of Virginia

Invited Speakers

Mirella Lapata, University of Edinburgh
Rada Mihalcea, University of Michigan, Ann Arbor
Nina Balcan, Carnegie Mellon University
Carlos Guestrin, Stanford University

Keynote Talk: Invited Talk 1

Mirella Lapata
School of Informatics, University of Edinburgh

Abstract: Invited Talk at the 2nd WIT: Workshop On Deriving Insights From User-Generated Text at ACL2022

Bio: Mirella Lapata is a professor in the School of Informatics at the University of Edinburgh. I'm affiliated with the Institute for Communicating and Collaborative Systems and the Edinburgh Natural Language Processing Group.
Her research focuses on computational models for the representation, extraction, and generation of semantic information from structured and unstructured data, involving text and other modalities such as images, video, and large scale knowledge bases. I have worked on a variety of applied NLP tasks such as semantic parsing and semantic role labeling, discourse coherence, summarization, text simplification, concept-to-text generation, and question answering. I have also used computational models (drawing mainly on probabilistic generative models) to explore aspects of human cognition such as learning concepts, judging similarity, forming perceptual representations, and learning word meanings. The overarching goal of my research is to enable computers to understand requests and act on them, process and aggregate large amounts of data, and convey information based on them. Critical for all these tasks are models for extracting and representing meaning from natural language text, storing meanings internally, and working with stored meanings to derive further consequences.

Keynote Talk: Invited 2

Rada Mihalcea
University of Michigan, Ann Arbor

Abstract: Invited Talk at the 2nd WIT: Workshop On Deriving Insights From User-Generated Text at ACL2022

Bio: Rada Mihalcea is the Janice M. Jenkins Collegiate Professor of Computer Science and Engineering at the University of Michigan and the Director of the Michigan Artificial Intelligence Lab. Her research interests are in computational linguistics, with a focus on lexical semantics, multilingual natural language processing, and computational social sciences. She serves or has served on the editorial boards of the Journals of Computational Linguistics, Language Resources and Evaluations, Natural Language Engineering, Journal of Artificial Intelligence Research, IEEE Transactions on Affective Computing, and Transactions of the Association for Computational Linguistics. She was a program co-chair for EMNLP 2009 and ACL 2011, and a general chair for NAACL 2015 and *SEM 2019. She currently serves as ACL President. She is the recipient of a Presidential Early Career Award for Scientists and Engineers awarded by President Obama (2009), an ACM Fellow (2019) and a AAAI Fellow (2021). In 2013, she was made an honorary citizen of her hometown of Cluj-Napoca, Romania.

Keynote Talk: Invited 3

Nina Balcan
Carnegie Mellon University

Abstract: Invited Talk at the 2nd WIT: Workshop On Deriving Insights From User-Generated Text at ACL2022

Bio: Maria-Florina (Nina) Balcan is the Cadence Design Systems Professor of Computer Science at the School of Computer Science (MLD and CSD) at Carnegie Mellon University, she is also Sloan Fellow and Microsoft Faculty Fellow. Nina's main research interests are in machine learning, artificial intelligence, and theoretical computer science. Current research focus includes developing foundations and principled, practical algorithms for important modern learning paradigms. These include interactive learning, distributed learning, learning representations, life-long learning, and metalearning. Her research addresses important challenges of these settings, including statistical efficiency, computational efficiency, noise tolerance, limited supervision or interaction, privacy, low communication, and incentives. Other research topics are i) Foundations and applications of data driven algorithm design. Design and analysis of algorithms on realistic instances (a.k.a. beyond worst case).; ii) Computational and data-driven approaches in game theory and economics; iii) computational, learning theoretic, and game theoretic aspects of multi-agent systems, and iv) Analyzing the overall behavior of complex systems in which multiple agents with limited information are adapting their behavior based on past experience, both in social and engineered systems contexts.

Keynote Talk: Invited 4

Carlos Guestrin
Stanford University

Abstract: Invited Talk at the 2nd WIT: Workshop On Deriving Insights From User-Generated Text at ACL2022

Bio: Carlos Guestrin is a Professor in the Computer Science Department at Stanford University. His previous positions include the Amazon Professor of Machine Learning at the Computer Science and Engineering Department of the University of Washington, the Finmeccanica Associate Professor at Carnegie Mellon University, and the Senior Director of Machine Learning and AI at Apple, after the acquisition of Turi, Inc. (formerly GraphLab and Dato) — Carlos co-founded Turi, which developed a platform for developers and data scientist to build and deploy intelligent applications. He is a technical advisor for OctoML.ai. His team also released a number of popular open-source projects, including XGBoost, LIME, Apache TVM, MXNet, Turi Create, GraphLab/PowerGraph, SFrame, and GraphChi.
Carlos received the IJCAI Computers and Thought Award and the Presidential Early Career Award for Scientists and Engineers (PECASE). He is also a recipient of the ONR Young Investigator Award, NSF Career Award, Alfred P. Sloan Fellowship, and IBM Faculty Fellowship, and was named one of the 2008 'Brilliant 10' by Popular Science Magazine. Carlos' work received awards at a number of conferences and journals, including ACL, AISTATS, ICML, IPSN, JAIR, JWRPM, KDD, NeurIPS, UAI, and VLDB. He is a former member of the Information Sciences and Technology (ISAT) advisory group for DARPA.

Table of Contents

Program

Friday, May 27, 2022

09:20 - 09:30	*Opening Remarks*
09:30 - 10:30	*Invited Talk I*
10:30 - 11:00	*Coffee Break*
11:00 - 11:30	*Session 1*
	An Interactive Analysis of User-reported Long COVID Symptoms using Twitter Data Lin Miao, Mark Last and Marina Litvak
	Bi-Directional Recurrent Neural Ordinary Differential Equations for Social Media Text Classification Maunika Tamire, Srinivas Anumasa and P. K. Srijith
12:30 - 11:30	*Invited Talk II*
12:30 - 14:00	*Lunch Break*
15:00 - 14:00	*Invited Talk III*
15:00 - 15:30	*Coffee Break*
15:30 - 15:45	*Session 2*
	Unsupervised Abstractive Dialogue Summarization with Word Graphs and POV Conversion Seongmin Park and Jihwa Lee
15:45 - 16:45	*Invited Talk IV*
16:45 - 17:45	*Panel*

Unsupervised Abstractive Dialogue Summarization with Word Graphs and POV Conversion

Seongmin Park, Jihwa Lee
ActionPower, Seoul, Republic of Korea
{seongmin.park, jihwa.lee}@actionopwer.kr

Abstract

We advance the state-of-the-art in unsupervised abstractive dialogue summarization by utilizing multi-sentence compression graphs. Starting from well-founded assumptions about word graphs, we present simple but reliable path-reranking and topic segmentation schemes. Robustness of our method is demonstrated on datasets across multiple domains, including meetings, interviews, movie scripts, and day-to-day conversations. We also identify possible avenues to augment our heuristic-based system with deep learning. We open-source our code[1], to provide a strong, reproducible baseline for future research into unsupervised dialogue summarization.

1 Introduction

Compared to traditional text summarization, dialogue summarization introduces a unique challenge: conversion of first- and second-person speech into third-person reported speech. Such discrepancy between the observed text and expected model output puts greater emphasis on abstractive transduction than in traditional summarization tasks. The disorientation is further exacerbated by each of many diverse dialogue types calling for a differing form of transduction – short dialogues require terse abstractions, while meeting transcripts require summaries by agenda.

Thus, despite the steady emergence of dialogue summarization datasets, the field of dialogue summarization is still bottlenecked by a scarcity of training data. To train a truly robust dialogue summarization model, one requires transcript-summary pairs not only across diverse *dialogue domains*, but also across multiple *dialogue types* as well. The lack of diverse annotated summarization data is especially pronounced in low-resourced languages. From such state of the literature, we identify a need for unsupervised dialogue summarization.

[1]https://github.com/seongminp/graph-dialogue-summary

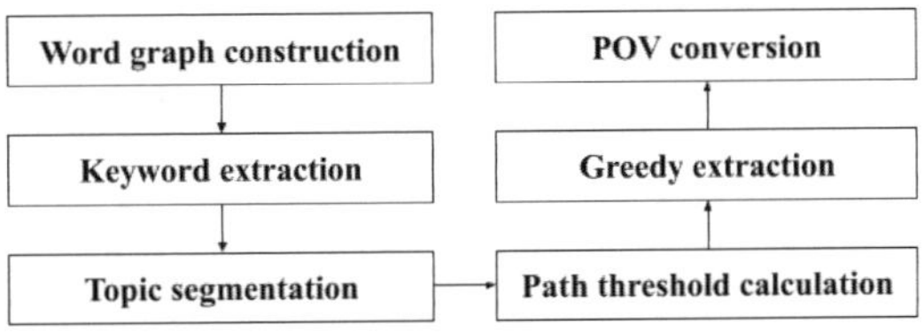

Figure 1: Our summarization pipeline.

Our method builds upon previous research on unsupervised summarization using word graphs. Starting from the simple assumption that *a good summary sentence is at least as informative as any single input sentence*, we develop novel schemes for path extraction from word graphs. Our contributions are as follows:

1. We present a novel scheme for path reranking in graph-based summarization. We show that, in practice, simple keyword counting performs better than complex baselines. For longer texts, we present an optional topic segmentation scheme.

2. We introduce a point-of-view (POV) conversion module to convert semi-extractive summaries into fully abstractive summaries. The new module by itself improves all scores on baseline methods, as well as our own.

3. Finally, We verify our model on datasets beyond those traditionally used in literature to provide a strong baseline for future research.

With just an off-the-shelf part-of-speech (POS) tagger and a list of stopwords, our model can be applied across different types of dialogue summarization.

2 Background

2.1 Multi-sentence compression graphs

Pioneered by Filippova (2010), a Multi-Sentence Compression Graph (MSCG) is a graph whose

Proceedings of the 2nd Workshop on Deriving Insights from User-Generated Text, pages 1 - 9
May 27, 2022 ©2022 Association for Computational Linguistics

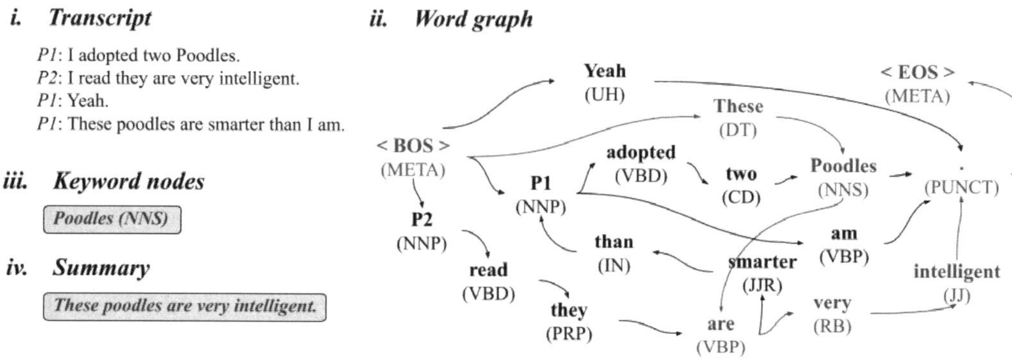

Figure 2: Construction of word graph. Red nodes and edges denote the selected summary path. Node highlighted in purple ("Poodles") is the only non-stopword node included in the k-core subgraph of the word graph. We use nodes from the k-core subgraph as keyword nodes. All original sentences from the unabridged input is present as a possible path from v_{bos} to v_{eos}. Paths that contain more information than those original paths are extracted as summaries.

nodes are words from the input text and edges are coocurrance statistics between adjacent words. During preprocessing, words “<bos>” (beginning-of-sentence) and “<eos>” (end-of-sentence) are prepended and appended, respectively, to every input sentence. Thus, all sentences from the input are represented in the graph as a single path from the *<bos>* node (v_{bos}) to the *<eos>* node (v_{eos}). Overlapping words among sentences will create intersecting paths within MSCG, creating new paths from v_{bos} to v_{eos}, unseen in the original text. Capturing these possibly shorter but informative paths is the key to performant summarization with MSCGs.

Ganesan et al. (2010) introduce an abstractive sentence generation method from word graphs to produce opinion summaries. Tixier et al. (2016) show that nodes with maximal neighbors – a concept captured by graph degeneracy – likely belong to important keywords of the document. Shortest paths from v_{bos} to v_{eos} are scored according to how many keyword nodes they contain. Subsequently, a budget-maximization scheme is introduced to find the set of paths that maximizes the score sum within designated word count (Tixier et al., 2017). We also adopt graph degeneracy to identify keyword nodes in MSCG.

2.2 Unsupervised Abstractive Dialogue Summarization

Aside from MSCGs, unsupervised dialogue summarization usually employ end-to-end neural architectures. Zhang et al. (2021) and Zou et al. (2021) utilize text variational autoencoders (VAEs) (Kingma and Welling, 2014; Bowman et al., 2016) to decode conditional or denoised abridgements. Fu et al. (2021) reformulate summary generation into a self-supervised task by equipping auxiliary objectives to the training architecture. Among end-to-end frameworks we only include Fu et al. (2021) as our baseline, because the brittle nature of training text VAEs, coupled with the lack of detail on data and parameters used to train the models, render VAE-based methods beyond reproducible.

3 Summarization strategy

In following subsections we outline our proposed summarization process.

3.1 Word graph construction

First, we assemble a word graph G from the input text. We use a modified version of Filippova (2010)'s algorithm for graph construction:

- Let SW be a set of stopwords and $T = s_0, s_1, ...$ be a sequence of sentences in the input text.

- Decompose all $s_i \in T$ into a sequence of POS-tagged words.

$$s_i = (\text{“}bos\text{”}, \text{“}meta\text{”}), (w_{i,0}, pos_{i,0}), ..., \\ (w_{i,n-1}, pos_{i,n-1}), (\text{“}eos\text{”}, \text{“}meta\text{”}) \quad (1)$$

- For every $(w_{i,j}, pos_{i,j}) \in s_i$ such that $w_i \notin SW$ and $s_i \in T$, add a node v in G. If a node v' with the same lowercase word $w_{i,k}$ and tag $pos_{i,k}$ such that $j \neq k$ exists, pair $(w_{i,j}, pos_{i,j})$ with v' instead of creating a new node. If multiple such matches exist, select the node with maximal overlapping context ($w_{i,j-1}$ and $w_{i,j+1}$).

- Add stopword nodes – $(w_{i,j}, pos_{i,j}) \in s_i$ such that $w_{i,j} \in SW$ and $s_i \in T$ – to G with the algorithm described above.

- For all $s_i \in T$, add a directed edge between node pairs that correspond to subsequent words. Edge weight w between nodes v_1 and v_2 is calculated as follows:

$$w' = \frac{freq(v_1) + freq(v_2)}{(\sum_{s_i \in T} diff(i, v_1, v_2))^{-1}} \quad (2)$$

$$w'' = freq(v_1) * freq(v_2) \quad (3)$$

$$w = w'/w'' \quad (4)$$

$freq(v)$ is the number of words from original text mapped to node v. $diff(i, v_1, v_2)$ is the absolute difference in word positions of v_1 and v_2 within s_i:

$$diff(i, v_1, v_2) = |k - j| \quad (5)$$

, where w_{ij} and w_{ik} are words in s_i that correspond to nodes v_1 and v_2, respectively.

In edge weight calculation, w' favors edges with strong cooccurrence, while w''^{-1} favors edges with greater salience, as measured by word frequency.

It follows from above that only a single <*bos*> node and a single <*eos*> node will exist once the graph is completed.

3.2 Keyword extraction

The resulting graph from the previous step is a composition that captures syntactic importance. Traditional approaches utilize centrality measures to identify important nodes within word graphs (Mihalcea and Tarau, 2004; Erkan and Radev, 2004). In this work we use graph degeneracy to extract keyword nodes. In a k-degenerate word graph, words that belong to k-core nodes of the graph are considered to be keywords. We collect KW, a set of nodes belonging to the k-core subgraph. The k-core of a graph is the maximally degenerate subgraph, with minimum degree of at least k.

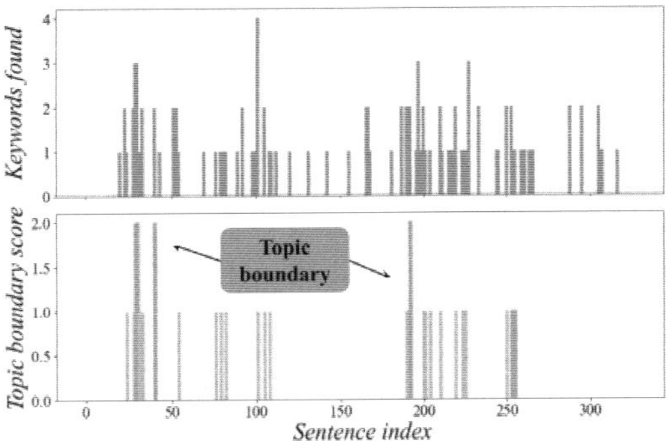

Figure 3: Topic segmentation on AMI meeting ID ES2005b. Green bars indicate sentence boundaries with highest topic distance.

3.3 Path threshold calculation

Once keyword nodes are identified, we score every path from v_{bos} to v_{eos} that corresponds to a sentence from the original text. Contrary to previous research into word-graph based summarization, we use a simple keyword coverage score for every path:

$$Score_i = \frac{|V_i \cap KW|}{|KW|} \quad (6)$$

, where V_i is the set of all nodes in path p_i, a representation of sentence $s_i \in T$, within the word graph. We calculate the path threshold t, the mean score of all sentences in the original text. Later, when summaries are extracted from the word graph, candidates with path score less than t are discarded. We also experimented with setting t as the minimum or maximum of all original path scores, but such configurations yielded inferior summaries influenced by outlier path scores.

Our path score function is reminiscent of the diversity reward function in Shang et al. (2018). However, we use the function as a measure of *coverage* instead of *diversity*. More importantly, we utilize the score as means to extract a threshold based on all input sentences, which is significantly different from Shang et al. (2018)'s utilization of the function as a monotonically increasing scorer in submodularity maximization.

3.4 Topic segmentation

For long texts, we apply an optional topic segmentation step. Our summarization algorithm is separately applied to each segmented text. Similar to path ranking in the next section, topics are determined according to keyword frequency. For every

Dataset	Domain	Test files	Dialogue length (chars)	Summary length (chars)
AMI	Meeting	20	22,499 (4,665 words)	1,808 (292 words)
ICSI	Meeting	6	42,484 (8,926 words)	2,271 (371 words)
DialogSum	Day-to-day	500	633 (125 words)	115 (19 words)
SAMSum	Day-to-day	819	414 (84 words)	109 (20 words)
MediaSum	Interview	10,000	8,718 (1,562 chars)	335 (59 words)
SummScreen	Screenplay	2,130	23,693 (5,642 words)	1,795 (342 words)
ADS	Debate	45	2918 (534 words)	882 (150 words)

Table 1: Statistics for benchmark datasets. All character-level and word-level statistics are averaged over the test set and rounded to the nearest whole number.

sentence in the input, we construct a *topic coverage* vector c, a zero-initialized row-vector of length $|KW|$. Each column of the row vector is a binary representation signaling the presence of a single element in KW. Topic coverage vector of a path containing two keywords from KW, for instance, would contain two columns with 1.

Every transition between sentences is a potential topic boundary. Since each sentence (and corresponding path) has an associated topic coverage vector, we quantify the topic distance d of a sentence with the next as the negative cosine distance of their topic vectors:

$$d_{i,i+1} = -\frac{c_i \cdot c_{i+1}}{\|c_i\| \|c_{i+1}\|} \quad (7)$$

If p is a hyperparameter representing the total number of topics, one can segment the original text at $p-1$ sentence boundaries with the greatest topic distance. Alternatively, sentence boundaries with topic distance greater than a designated threshold can be selected as topic boundaries. For simplicity, we proceed with the former segmentation setup (top-p boundary) when necessary.

3.5 Summary path extraction

We generate a summary per-speaker. Our construction of the word graph allows fast extraction of sub-graphs containing only nodes pertaining to utterances from a single speaker. For each speaker subgraph, we generate summary sentences as follows:

1. We obtain k shortest paths from v_{bos} to v_{eos} by applying the k-shortest paths algorithm (Yen, 1971) to our word graph.

2. Iterating from the shortest path, we collect any paths with keyword coverage score above the threshold calculated in 3.3.

3. For each path found, we track the set of encountered keywords in KW. We stop our search if all keywords in KW were encountered, or a pre-defined number of iterations (the search depth) is reached.

A good summary has to be both concise and informative. Intuitively, edge weights of the proposed word graph captures the former, while keyword thresholding prioritizes the latter.

3.6 POV conversion

Finally, we convert our collected semi-extractive summaries into abstractive reported speech using a rule-based POV conversion module. We describe sentences extracted from our word graph as *semi-extractive* rather than *extractive*, to recognize the distinction between previously unseen sentences created from pieces of text, and sentences taken verbatim from the original text. Similar to existing *extract-then-abstract* summarization pipelines (Mao et al., 2021; Liu et al., 2021), our method hinges on the assumption that the extractive path-reranking step will optimize for *summary content*, while the succeeding abstractive POV-conversion step will do so for *summary style*. FewSum (Bražinskas et al., 2020) also applies POV conversion in a few-shot summarization setting. FewSum conditions the summary generator to produce sentences in targeted styles, which is achieved by nudging the decoder to generate pronouns appropriate for each designated tone.

Popular literature has established that defining an all-encompassing set of rules for indirect speech conversion is infeasible (Partee, 1973; Li, 2011). In fact, the English grammar is mostly descriptive rather than prescriptive – no set of official rules dictated by a single governing authority exists. Even so, rule based POV conversion does provide a strong baseline compared to state-of-the-art

Model	AMI			ICSI		
	R1	R2	RL	R1	R2	RL
RepSum Fu et al. (2021)	18.88	2.38	15.62	-	-	-
Filippova (2010)	33.47	6.21	15.15	26.53	3.69	12.09
Mehdad et al. (2013)	34.62	6.49	15.41	27.20	3.57	12.55
Boudin and Morin (2013)	34.21	6.37	14.92	26.90	3.64	12.18
Shang et al. (2018)	34.34	6.13	15.58	26.93	3.65	12.68
Filippova (2010) $_{+POV}$	34.16	6.35	15.27	26.79	3.81	12.21
Mehdad et al. (2013) $_{+POV}$	**35.39**	6.59	15.54	27.48	3.65	12.66
Boudin and Morin (2013) $_{+POV}$	34.93	6.49	15.07	27.14	3.72	12.20
Shang et al. (2018) $_{+POV}$	34.91	6.18	**15.70**	27.27	3.72	**12.78**
Ours $_{PreSeg}$	32.21	5.55	14.85	27.60	4.43	11.66
Ours $_{TopicSeg}$	33.30	6.59	14.19	27.66	4.27	12.16
Ours $_{PreSeg+POV}$	33.66	**6.85**	14.17	27.80	**4.56**	11.77
Ours $_{TopicSeg+POV}$	33.21	5.84	15.30	**27.84**	4.33	12.29

Table 2: Results on meeting summarization datasets. All reported scores are F-1 measures. Models with POV indicate post-proceessing with our suggested POV conversion module. $PreSeg$ models utilize topic segmentations provided in Shang et al. (2018), and $TopicSeg$ models intake unsegmented raw transcripts and perform the topic segmentation algorithm suggested in this paper. Results for RepSum are quoted from the original paper.

techniques, such as end-to-end Transformer networks (Lee et al., 2020). In this study, we limit our scope to rule-based conversion because only the rule-based system among all tested methods in Lee et al. (2020) confers to the unsupervised nature of this paper. We encourage further research into integrating more advanced reported speech conversion techniques into the abstractive summarization pipeline.

In this work, we apply four conversion rules:

1. Change pronouns from first person to third person.
2. Change modal verbs *can*, *may*, and *must* to *could*, *might*, and *had to*, respectively.
3. Convert questions into a pre-defined template: *<Speaker> asks <utterance>*.
4. Fix subject-verb agreement after applying rules above.

We notably omit prepend rules suggested in (Lee et al., 2020), because the input domain of our summarization system is unbounded, unlike with task-oriented spoken commands for virtual assistants. We also leave tense conversion for future research.

4 Experiments

4.1 Datasets

We test our model on dialogue summarization datasets across multiple domains:

1. Meetings: *AMI* (McCowan et al., 2005), *ICSI* (Janin et al., 2003)
2. Day-to-day conversations: *DialogSum* (Chen et al., 2021b), *SAMSum* (Gliwa et al., 2019)
3. Interview: *MediaSum* (Zhu et al., 2021)
4. Screenplay: *SummScreen* (Chen et al., 2021a)
5. Debate: *ADS* (Fabbri et al., 2021)

Table 1 provides detailed statistics and descriptions for each dataset.

For AMI and ICSI, we conduct several ablation experiments with different components of our model omitted: semi-extractive summarization without POV conversion is compared with fully-abstractive summarization with POV conversion; utilization of pre-segmented text provided by Shang et al. (2018) is compared with application of topic segmentation suggested in this paper.

4.2 Baselines

For meeting summaries, we compare our method with previous research on unsupervised dialogue summarization. Along with Filippova (2010), Shang et al. (2018), and Fu et al. (2021), we select Boudin and Morin (2013) and Mehdad et al. (2013) as our baselines. All but Fu et al. (2021) are word graph-based summarizers.

For all other categories, we choose LEAD-3 as our unsupervised baseline. LEAD-3 selects the

Dataset	Our results			LEAD-3		
	R1	R2	RL	R1	R2	RL
DialogSum	**20.79**	5.43	15.14	19.46	**6.19**	**15.99**
SAMSum	**26.48**	**9.69**	**19.65**	21.93	8.52	18.65
MediaSum	7.19	1.79	5.66	**8.58**	**3.19**	**6.62**
SummScreen	**21.25**	**2.23**	**9.40**	5.18	0.55	3.75
ADS	**28.00**	**7.33**	**14.75**	19.39	5.72	13.22

Table 3: Results on day-to-day, interview, screenplay, and debate summarization datasets. All reported scores are F-1 measures. In our method, topic segmentation is applied to datasets with average transcription length greater than 5,000 characters (MediaSum, SummScreen), and POV conversion is applied to all datasets.

first three sentences of a document as the summary. Because summary distributions in several document types tend to be front-heavy (Grenander et al., 2019; Zhu et al., 2021), LEAD-3 provides a competitive extractive baseline with negligible computational burden.

4.3 Evaluation

We evaluate the quality of generated system summaries against reference summaries using standard ROUGE scores (Lin, 2004). Specifically, we use ROUGE-1 ($R1$), ROUGE-2 ($R2$), and ROUGE-L (RL) scores that respectively measure unigram, bigram, and longest common subsequence coverage.

5 Results

5.1 Meeting summarization

Table 2 records experimental results on AMI and ISCI datasets. In all categories, our method or a baseline augmented with our POV conversion module outperforms previous state-of-the-art.

5.1.1 Effect of suggested path reranking

Our proposed path-reranking without POV conversion yields semi-extractive output summaries competitive with abstractive summarization baselines. Segmenting raw transcripts into topic groups with our method generally yields higher F-measures than using pre-segmented transcripts in semi-extractive summarization.

5.1.2 Effect of topic segmentation

Summarizing pre-segmented dialogue transcripts results in higher $R2$, while applying our topic segmentation method results in higher $R1$ and RL. This observation is in line with our method's emphasis on keyword extraction, in contrast to keyphrase extraction seen in several baselines (Boudin and Morin, 2013; Shang et al., 2018). Models that preserve *token adjacency* achieve higher $R2$, while models that preserve *token presence* achieve higher $R1$. RL additionally penalizes for wrong token order, but token order in extracted summaries tend to be well-preserved in word graph-based summarization schemes.

5.1.3 Effect of POV conversion module

Our POV conversion module improves benchmark scores on all tested baselines, as well as on our own system. It is only natural that a conversion module that translates text from semi-extractive to abstractive will raise scores on abstractive benchmarks. However, applying our POV module to *already abstractive* summarization systems resulted in higher scores in all cases. We attribute this to the fact that previous abstractive summarization systems do not generate sufficiently reportive summaries; past research either emphasize other linguistic aspects like hyponym conversion (Shang et al., 2018), or treat POV conversion as a byproduct of an end-to-end summarization pipeline (Fu et al., 2021).

5.2 Day-to-day, interview, screenplay, and debate summarization

Our method outperforms the LEAD-3 baseline on most benchmarks (Table 3). The model shows consistent performance across multiple domains in $R1$ and RL, but shows greater inconsistency in $R2$. Variance in the latter metric can be attributed, as in 5.1.2, to our model's tendency to optimize for single keywords rather than keyphrases. Robustness of our model, as measured by consistency of ROUGE measures across multiple datasets, is shown in Figure 4.

Notably, our method falters in the MediaSum benchmark. Compared to other benchmarks, MediaSum's reference summaries display heavy positional bias towards the beginning of its transcripts, which benefits the LEAD-3 approach. It also is the only dataset in which references summaries are

Transcript	Summary
Maya: Bring home the clothes that are hanging outside *Maya: All of them should be dry already and it looks like it's going to rain* *Boris: I'm not home right now* *Boris: I'll tell Brian to take care of that* *Maya: Fine, thanks*	*bring home the clothes that are hanging outside* *boris 'll tell brian to take care of that*
Keywords: 'care', 'clothes', 'home', 'thanks'	
Megan: Are we going to take a taxi to the opera? *Joseph: No, I'll take my car.* *Megan: Great, more convenient*	*are we going to take a taxi to the opera ?* *no , joseph 'll take my car*
Keywords: 'car', 'convenient', 'taxi', 'opera'	
Anne: You were right, he was lying to me :/ *Irene: Oh no, what happened?* *Jane: who?* *Jane: that Mark guy?* *Anne: yeah, he told me he's 30, today I saw his passport - he's 40* *Irene: You sure it's so important?* *Anne: he lied to me Irene*	*he lied to me he 's 30 , today anne saw his passport - he 's 40 yeah , he told me* *oh no , what happened? who ?* *annerene he lied to me : /*
Keywords: 'guy', '/', 'passport', 'yeah', 'today'	

Table 4: Summarizing the SAMSum corpus (Gliwa et al., 2019).

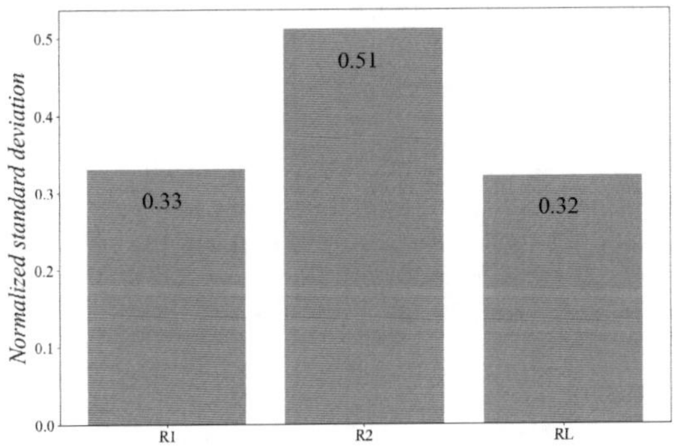

Figure 4: Normalized standard deviation (also called coefficient of variance) of R1, R2, and RL scores across all datasets. Normalized standard deviation is calculated as $\sigma/\bar{x}$, where σ is the standard deviation and $\bar{x}$ is the mean.

not generated for the purpose of summary evaluation, but are scraped from source news providers. Reference summaries for MediaSum utilize less reported speech compared to other datasets, and thus our POV module fails to boost the precision of summaries generated by our model.

6 Conclusion

6.1 Improving MSCG summarization

This paper improves upon previous work on multi-sentence compression graphs for summarization. We find that simpler and more adaptive path reranking schemes can boost summarization quality. We also demonstrate a promising possibility for integrating point-of-view conversion into summarization pipelines.

Compared to previous research, our model is still insufficient in keyphrase or bigram preservation. This phenomenon is captured by inconsistent $R2$ scores across benchmarks. We believe incorporating findings from keyphrase-based summarizers (Riedhammer et al., 2010; Boudin and Morin, 2013) can mitigate such shortcomings.

6.2 Avenues for future research

While our methods demonstrate improved benchmark results, its mostly heuristic nature leaves much room for enhancement through integration of statistical models. POV conversion in particular can benefit from deep learning-based approaches (Lee et al., 2020). With recent advances in unsupervised sequence to sequence transduction (Li et al.,

2020; He et al., 2020), we expect further research into more advanced POV conversion techniques will improve unsupervised dialogue summarization.

Another possibility to augment our research with deep learning is through employing graph networks (Cui et al., 2020) for representing MSCGs. With graph networks, each word node and edge can be represented as a contextualized vector. Such schemes will enable a more flexible and interpolatable manipulation of syntax captured by traditional word graphs.

One notable shortcoming of our system is the generation of summaries that lack grammatical coherence or fluency (Table 4). We intentionally leave out complex path filters that gauge linguistic validity or factual correctness. We only minimally inspect our summaries to check for inclusion of verb nodes, as in Filippova (2010). Our system can be easily augmented with such additional filters, which we leave for future work.

References

Florian Boudin and Emmanuel Morin. 2013. Keyphrase extraction for n-best reranking in multi-sentence compression. In *North American Chapter of the Association for Computational Linguistics (NAACL)*.

Samuel R. Bowman, Luke Vilnis, Oriol Vinyals, Andrew Dai, Rafal Jozefowicz, and Samy Bengio. 2016. Generating sentences from a continuous space. In *Proceedings of The 20th SIGNLL Conference on Computational Natural Language Learning*, pages 10–21, Berlin, Germany. Association for Computational Linguistics.

Arthur Bražinskas, Mirella Lapata, and Ivan Titov. 2020. Few-shot learning for opinion summarization. In *Proceedings of the 2020 Conference on Empirical Methods in Natural Language Processing (EMNLP)*, pages 4119–4135, Online. Association for Computational Linguistics.

Mingda Chen, Zewei Chu, Sam Wiseman, and Kevin Gimpel. 2021a. Summscreen: A dataset for abstractive screenplay summarization. *arXiv preprint arXiv:2104.07091*.

Yulong Chen, Yang Liu, and Yue Zhang. 2021b. Dialogsum challenge: Summarizing real-life scenario dialogues. In *Proceedings of the 14th International Conference on Natural Language Generation*, pages 308–313.

Peng Cui, Le Hu, and Yuanchao Liu. 2020. Enhancing extractive text summarization with topic-aware graph neural networks. In *Proceedings of the 28th International Conference on Computational Linguistics*, pages 5360–5371, Barcelona, Spain (Online). International Committee on Computational Linguistics.

Günes Erkan and Dragomir R Radev. 2004. Lexrank: Graph-based lexical centrality as salience in text summarization. *Journal of artificial intelligence research*, 22:457–479.

Alexander Fabbri, Faiaz Rahman, Imad Rizvi, Borui Wang, Haoran Li, Yashar Mehdad, and Dragomir Radev. 2021. ConvoSumm: Conversation summarization benchmark and improved abstractive summarization with argument mining. In *Proceedings of the 59th Annual Meeting of the Association for Computational Linguistics and the 11th International Joint Conference on Natural Language Processing (Volume 1: Long Papers)*, pages 6866–6880, Online. Association for Computational Linguistics.

Katja Filippova. 2010. Multi-sentence compression: Finding shortest paths in word graphs. In *Proceedings of the 23rd International Conference on Computational Linguistics (Coling 2010)*, pages 322–330, Beijing, China. Coling 2010 Organizing Committee.

Xiyan Fu, Yating Zhang, Tianyi Wang, Xiaozhong Liu, Changlong Sun, and Zhenglu Yang. 2021. Repsum: Unsupervised dialogue summarization based on replacement strategy. In *Proceedings of the 59th Annual Meeting of the Association for Computational Linguistics and the 11th International Joint Conference on Natural Language Processing (Volume 1: Long Papers)*, pages 6042–6051.

Kavita Ganesan, ChengXiang Zhai, and Jiawei Han. 2010. Opinosis: A graph based approach to abstractive summarization of highly redundant opinions. In *Proceedings of the 23rd International Conference on Computational Linguistics (Coling 2010)*, pages 340–348, Beijing, China. Coling 2010 Organizing Committee.

Bogdan Gliwa, Iwona Mochol, Maciej Biesek, and Aleksander Wawer. 2019. SAMSum corpus: A human-annotated dialogue dataset for abstractive summarization. In *Proceedings of the 2nd Workshop on New Frontiers in Summarization*, pages 70–79, Hong Kong, China. Association for Computational Linguistics.

Matt Grenander, Yue Dong, Jackie Chi Kit Cheung, and Annie Louis. 2019. Countering the effects of lead bias in news summarization via multi-stage training and auxiliary losses. In *Proceedings of the 2019 Conference on Empirical Methods in Natural Language Processing and the 9th International Joint Conference on Natural Language Processing (EMNLP-IJCNLP)*, pages 6019–6024, Hong Kong, China. Association for Computational Linguistics.

Junxian He, Xinyi Wang, Graham Neubig, and Taylor Berg-Kirkpatrick. 2020. A probabilistic formulation of unsupervised text style transfer. In *International Conference on Learning Representations*.

Adam Janin, Don Baron, Jane Edwards, Dan Ellis, David Gelbart, Nelson Morgan, Barbara Peskin, Thilo Pfau, Elizabeth Shriberg, Andreas Stolcke, et al. 2003. The icsi meeting corpus. In *2003 IEEE International Conference on Acoustics, Speech, and Signal Processing, 2003. Proceedings.(ICASSP'03).*, volume 1, pages I–I. IEEE.

Diederik P. Kingma and Max Welling. 2014. Auto-encoding variational bayes. In *2nd International Conference on Learning Representations, ICLR 2014, Banff, AB, Canada, April 14-16, 2014, Conference Track Proceedings*.

Gunhee Lee, Vera Zu, Sai Srujana Buddi, Dennis Liang, Purva Kulkarni, and Jack FitzGerald. 2020. Converting the point of view of messages spoken to virtual assistants. In *Findings of the Association for Computational Linguistics: EMNLP 2020*, pages 154–163, Online. Association for Computational Linguistics.

Charles N Li. 2011. Direct speech and indirect speech: A functional study. In *Direct and indirect speech*, pages 29–46. De Gruyter Mouton.

Chunyuan Li, Xiang Gao, Yuan Li, Xiujun Li, Baolin Peng, Yizhe Zhang, and Jianfeng Gao. 2020. Optimus: Organizing sentences via pre-trained modeling of a latent space. In *EMNLP*.

Chin-Yew Lin. 2004. ROUGE: A package for automatic evaluation of summaries. In *Text Summarization Branches Out*, pages 74–81, Barcelona, Spain. Association for Computational Linguistics.

Wenfeng Liu, Yaling Gao, Jinming Li, and Yuzhen Yang. 2021. A combined extractive with abstractive model for summarization. *IEEE Access*, 9:43970–43980.

Ziming Mao, Chen Henry Wu, Ansong Ni, Yusen Zhang, Rui Zhang, Tao Yu, Budhaditya Deb, Chenguang Zhu, Ahmed H Awadallah, and Dragomir Radev. 2021. Dyle: Dynamic latent extraction for abstractive long-input summarization. *arXiv preprint arXiv:2110.08168*.

Iain McCowan, Jean Carletta, Wessel Kraaij, Simone Ashby, S Bourban, M Flynn, M Guillemot, Thomas Hain, J Kadlec, Vasilis Karaiskos, et al. 2005. The ami meeting corpus. In *Proceedings of the 5th international conference on methods and techniques in behavioral research*, volume 88, page 100. Citeseer.

Yashar Mehdad, Giuseppe Carenini, Frank Tompa, and Raymond Ng. 2013. Abstractive meeting summarization with entailment and fusion. In *Proceedings of the 14th European Workshop on Natural Language Generation*, pages 136–146.

Rada Mihalcea and Paul Tarau. 2004. TextRank: Bringing order into text. In *Proceedings of the 2004 Conference on Empirical Methods in Natural Language Processing*, pages 404–411, Barcelona, Spain. Association for Computational Linguistics.

Barbara Partee. 1973. The syntax and semantics of quotation. In S. R. Anderson and P. Kiparsky, editors, *A Festschrift for Morris Halle*, pages 410–418. New York: Holt, Reinehart and Winston.

Korbinian Riedhammer, Benoit Favre, and Dilek Hakkani-Tür. 2010. Long story short–global unsupervised models for keyphrase based meeting summarization. *Speech Communication*, 52(10):801–815.

Guokan Shang, Wensi Ding, Zekun Zhang, Antoine Jean-Pierre Tixier, Polykarpos Meladianos, Michalis Vazirgiannis, and Jean-Pierre Lorré. 2018. Unsupervised abstractive meeting summarization with multi-sentence compression and budgeted submodular maximization. *arXiv preprint arXiv:1805.05271*.

Antoine Tixier, Fragkiskos Malliaros, and Michalis Vazirgiannis. 2016. A graph degeneracy-based approach to keyword extraction. In *Proceedings of the 2016 conference on empirical methods in natural language processing*, pages 1860–1870.

Antoine Tixier, Polykarpos Meladianos, and Michalis Vazirgiannis. 2017. Combining graph degeneracy and submodularity for unsupervised extractive summarization. In *Proceedings of the workshop on new frontiers in summarization*, pages 48–58.

Jin Y Yen. 1971. Finding the k shortest loopless paths in a network. *management Science*, 17(11):712–716.

Xinyuan Zhang, Ruiyi Zhang, Manzil Zaheer, and Amr Ahmed. 2021. Unsupervised abstractive dialogue summarization for tete-a-tetes. *Proceedings of the AAAI Conference on Artificial Intelligence*, 35(16):14489–14497.

Chenguang Zhu, Yang Liu, Jie Mei, and Michael Zeng. 2021. MediaSum: A large-scale media interview dataset for dialogue summarization. In *Proceedings of the 2021 Conference of the North American Chapter of the Association for Computational Linguistics: Human Language Technologies*, pages 5927–5934, Online. Association for Computational Linguistics.

Yicheng Zou, Jun Lin, Lujun Zhao, Yangyang Kang, Zhuoren Jiang, Changlong Sun, Qi Zhang, Xuanjing Huang, and Xiaozhong Liu. 2021. Unsupervised summarization for chat logs with topic-oriented ranking and context-aware auto-encoders. *Proceedings of the AAAI Conference on Artificial Intelligence*, 35(16):14674–14682.

An Interactive Analysis of User-reported Long COVID Symptoms using Twitter Data

Lin Miao[1], Mark Last[1], Marina Litvak[2]
Ben-Gurion University of the Negev[1], Shamoon College of Engineering[2]
P.O.B. 653 Beer-Sheva 8410501 Israel[1], 56 Bialik St. Beer-Sheva 8410802 Israel[2]
miaol@post.bgu.ac.il, mlast@bgu.ac.il, litvak.marina@gmail.com

Abstract

With millions of documented recoveries from COVID-19 worldwide, various long-term sequelae have been observed in a large group of survivors. This paper is aimed at systematically analyzing user-generated conversations on Twitter that are related to long-term COVID symptoms for a better understanding of the Long COVID health consequences. Using an interactive information extraction tool built especially for this purpose, we extracted key information from the relevant tweets and analyzed the user-reported Long COVID symptoms with respect to their demographic and geographical characteristics. The results of our analysis are expected to improve the public awareness on long-term COVID-19 sequelae and provide important insights to public health authorities.

1 Introduction

The COVID-19 pandemic has affected millions of people all over the world. Despite the growing knowledge of COVID-19, much still remains unclear, especially potential long-term health consequences.

The term of Long COVID was brought up by the patients on Twitter in May 2020, in order to express their long-term COVID illness (Callard and Perego, 2021). Many Long COVID sufferers shared their persistent symptoms on social media bringing numerous discussions of similar symptoms experienced by others. Long COVID, also known as post COVID-19 syndrome, has no strict definition. The CDC of the United States[1] describes Long COVID as symptoms for four or more weeks after the infection, however, WHO[2] and British National Institute for Health and Care Excellence (NICE)[3] suggest three months after onset of COVID-19.

Though the majority of infected people experience mild symptoms with no necessity of hospitalization, the post-COVID syndrome is being reported by not just hospitalized patients. Therefore, massive user-generated Long COVID data available on social media has a significant value for tracking and analyzing the long-term syndrome.

Thus, in this work, we aim to apply Natural Language Processing (NLP) approaches to explore the characteristics of Long COVID symptoms reported by the Twitter users in terms of the patient gender, age, and location, as well as in terms of the symptoms duration. By extracting and analyzing key information from Long COVID-related tweets, we can discover less known chronic physical or mental conditions experienced by large groups of COVID-19 patients, and explore the relations between symptoms and demographic or geographic characteristics of patients. Moreover, we also seek to study the Long COVID evolution over time. To address this need, we compare the results of datasets collected in different time periods.

As part of this study, we developed an online dashboard[4] to visualize the analysis of Long COVID symptoms harvested from Twitter. A snapshot is shown in Fig. 1. This interactive dashboard provides multi-scale information and insights.

Our contributions can be summarized as follows:

- We build and publish two repositories of Long COVID-related tweets, which include user-generated reports on Long COVID experience from different periods of time[5].
- We conduct a comprehensive analysis of the

[1]https://www.cdc.gov/coronavirus/2019-ncov/long-term-effects/index.html?CDC_AA_refVal=https%3A%2F%2Fwww.%cdc.gov%2Fcoronavirus%2F2019-ncov%2Flong-term-effects.html

[2]https://www.who.int/publications/i/item/WHO-2019-nCoV-Post_COVID-19_condition-Clinical_case_definition-2021.1

[3]https://www.nice.org.uk/news/article/nice-rcgp-and-sign-publish-guideline-on-managing-the-long-term-effects-of-covid-19

[4]https://longcovid-dashboard.herokuapp.com/

[5]https://github.com/Lin1202/Longcoivd/blob/main/ long-covid_tweets.tar

Proceedings of the 2nd Workshop on Deriving Insights from User-Generated Text, pages 10 - 19

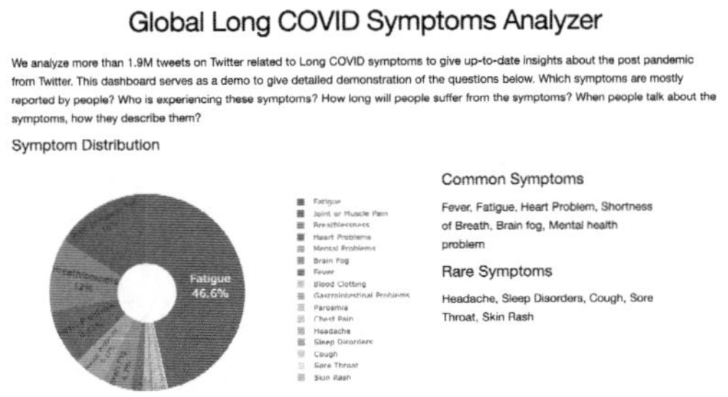

Figure 1: Snapshot of the dashboard

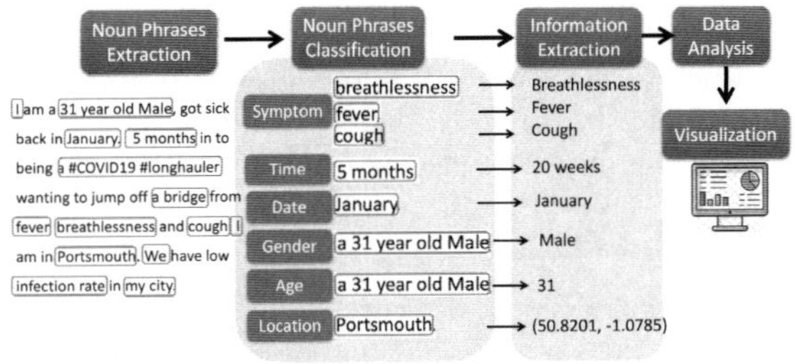

Figure 2: Methodology pipeline using synthetic data example

generated Long COVID datasets, which can provide insights to decision-makers and researchers.

- We explore several noun phrase classification models for information extraction from tweets to accurately recognize the long-term sequelae.
- We develop an online dashboard for interactive analysis of Long COVID symptoms from different perspectives.

2 Related Work

In response to the COVID-19 pandemic, extensive research has been conducted to help the healthcare community respond to this unprecedented emergency. As the concerns of COVID-19 long-term consequences are rising, more efforts are being invested in this topic. Current research about Long COVID uses standardized questionnaires or medical assessment to follow up the long-term symptoms of patients with clinical records (Carfì et al., 2020; Blomberg et al., 2021). Due to the lack of sufficient data about long-term COVID-19 complications, some studies explore the COVID-19 sequelae through the review of earlier papers (Mitrani et al., 2020; Kumar et al., 2021; Willi et al., 2021).

Numerous studies are using NLP approaches to contribute to the global response to this pandemic crisis. For instance, Silverman et al. (2021) use NLP pipeline to extract COVID symptoms from unstructured notes. With the use of NLP algorithms, Cury et al. (2021) assess the CT imaging reports for tracking of COVID-19 pandemic in the United States.

Data from social media is widely used for COVID symptom analysis (Sarker et al., 2020; Krittanawong et al., 2020). However, very few studies focus on Long COVID with social media attributes. Singh and Reddy (2020) and Banda et al. (2020) analyzed the long-term symptoms distribution by mining and manually reviewing tweets of around 100 self-reporting users. Sarker and Ge (2021) analyzed the major Long COVID symptoms distribution by extracting symptoms from posts on Reddit, using approximate matching approach based on an expanded meta-lexicon. They mainly analyzed the major symptoms distribution.

In this work, we utilize various NLP approaches to explore the Long COVID symptoms reported on Twitter. We aim to conduct multi-scale analysis of Long COVID symptoms, including not only the symptoms distribution and duration but also the effect of demographic and geographical patient characteristics.

3 Methodology

Our data analysis pipeline is demonstrated in Fig. 2, using a synthetic tweet based on several real tweets as an example. First, noun phrases (NPs) are identified in each tweet and then classified to different categories. Next, Long COVID-related information is extracted from the identified NPs for further analysis.

3.1 Noun Phrase Classification

We extract relevant information from tweets by identifying NPs from seven categories, as shown in Table 1. As observed, some NPs may carry more than one information category. For example, "my 31 year old daughter" contains 'age', and 'gender.' As such, we regard the NPs classification as a multi-label and multi-class classification task. After manually labeling some data, we aim to train a supervised classification model. In this work, we evaluate and compare the following NP classification models: (a) Support vector machine (SVM);

(b) Bidirectional Gated Recurrent Unit (GRU); (c) Bidirectional Encoder Representations from Transformers (BERT) (Devlin et al., 2019). The most accurate model is selected for this stage.

3.2 Information Extraction

After identifying NPs implicating valuable information, we process and extract information from these NPs for further analysis.

Symptom Categorization At this stage, we try to identify symptom-related NPs. The symptom classification task needs to capture the synonyms for each symptom category. Because text on Twitter is informal, the symptoms are not named in a consistent or complete way. We chose to overcome this problem using BERT embeddings. BERT is not only capable of providing similar embeddings for close meanings, it also gives contextualised embeddings. Additionally, as a Masked Language Model, BERT produces significant results in understanding an incomplete text. Therefore, we built the classification model by fine-tuning BERT to identify all the symptom-related NPs.

Gender Extraction We label NPs as "Gender" if they include gender information about the reported person, such as, "my daughter", "my husband". Also, some self-reported tweets mention the gender explicitly. We extract the patient gender ("male" or "female") from the relevant NPs by conducting binary classification.

Symptom Duration Calculation Considering the different definitions for Long COVID, we chose to use 'week' to measure the duration of the symptoms. It is observed that the users may report the time period of their Long COVID symptoms or the date of diagnosis, both of which can provide the duration of the symptoms. Therefore, we extract the symptom duration from NPs labeled as "Time" or "Date". The NPs classified as "Time", which are representing the time period, are converted into weeks directly. As for the NPs of "Date" category, which are expressing the date of the reported diagnosis, the duration is calculated by subtracting the creation date of the tweets.

Age Extraction The user age in years is extracted from the NPs assigned to the "Age" category by converting number text to integers and extracting the integers. Any extracted values that are out of age range ([0,100]) are then filtered out.

Location Process The geolocation information considers "Location" NPs and the reported locations in account profiles. However, if the geolocation information retrieved from the NP and the account profile are nonidentical for a single tweet, we keep the geolocation information from the NP. Later, the location information is converted into coordinates.

3.3 Data Analysis

In this work, we conduct analysis of three categories: demographic analysis, geographical analysis, and textual content analysis.

Demographic Analysis We analyze the distribution of the reported symptoms. Aligning the creation date of the tweets and the mentioned symptoms, we explore how the symptom distributions evolve through the timeline. To explore the associations of other features with symptoms, we associate the extracted information with the symptoms mentioned in the same tweet. Associated with gender information, we analyze the gender distribution of symptoms, to compare the symptoms experienced by men and women. Associated with gender and age/duration, we also present the joint distributions of gender, age/duration and several major symptoms respectively. The average age and duration of each symptom are calculated and demonstrated.

Geographical Analysis We visualize the locations on a global map, marked for different symptoms. The distribution of each symptom can be clearly seen on the map, providing a geographical perspective.

Textual Content Analysis To drill down into the tweets content, we generate a word cloud for the data of each month. The word cloud presents the most frequent words related to symptoms. Word cloud could enable to discover new symptoms and the interaction of several different symptoms. We use word distance with symptom words to filter out the frequent words that are irrelevant to Long COVID. Each word is represented by a word2vec vector. For each word, we calculate the distance to each vector in the symptom list, then keep the closest distance as the score for this word. Later, we sort these words by their scores from closest to farthest. The top 100 words are used for generating the word cloud.

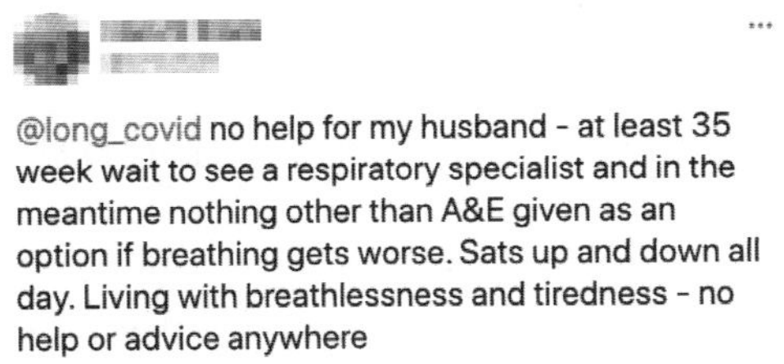

(a) Example 1

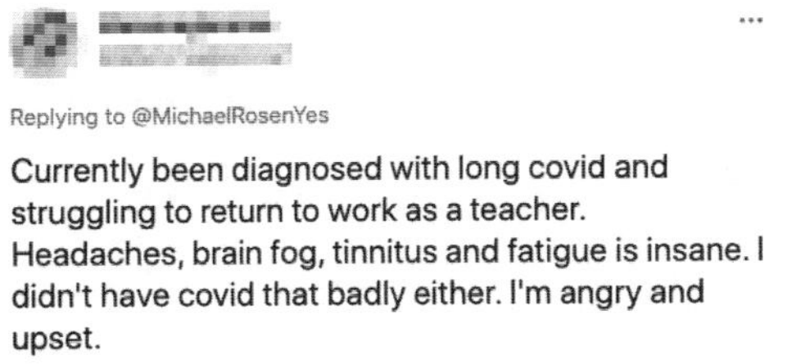

(b) Example 2

Figure 3: Examples of Long COVID-related tweets

4 Case Study

Based on the proposed pipeline, we conducted in-depth analysis of Long COVID symptoms reported on Twitter using a sample of Long COVID-related tweets between May to December 2020, and a sample of October 2021. To explore the Long COVID evolution over time, we compared the results of May-December 2020 and October 2021.

4.1 Data

Leveraging Twitter's streaming API, Chen et al. (2020) are using keywords to continuously collect a significant amount of COVID-19 tweets and periodically release it for research use. We used specific keywords (shown in Appendix A.1) to retrieve relevant tweets about Long COVID symptoms from this public coronavirus twitter dataset. We built two datasets: one is containing Long COVID-related tweets from 1st May to 31st December 2020; the other one is containing Long COVID-related tweets of October 2021. After removing non-English tweets and duplicates, our two datasets contain 2.3M relevant tweets, in which the amount is approximately 3.2% of the original dataset for the same period of time. Some Long COVID tweet examples are shown Fig. 3. Using keyword-based approach to gather tweets might exclude some relevant ones because of missing certain keywords or misspellings (as tweets are notoriously noisy). To estimate the False Negative (ratio of missing tweets) in our collection, we

Category	Description	#Labeled
Symptom	symptoms reported in tweets	340
Time	time period mentioned in tweets	179
Date	date mentioned in tweets	68
Age	age reported in tweets	44
Gender	gender reported in tweets	30
Location	location reported in tweets	45
None	none of the above	436

Table 1: Noun phrase categories and labeled data for NPs classification

manually verified 1432 tweets randomly selected from the original COVID-19 dataset. As a result, we got True Positive Rate of 78.8%, finding only two Long COVID-related tweets, which were missing in our collection. Hence, we may assume that our keyword-based approach with only 0.1% False Negative Rate is sufficient to cover most relevant tweets from the source dataset.

4.2 Noun Phrases Extraction and Classification

We used spaCy[6] for extracting the NPs from each tweet.

For NPs classification, one of the authors manually labeled a small subset of data from the 2020 dataset for training a supervised classification model. The details of the labeled data are shown in Table 1. The labeled data was randomly split into training and testing sets (80/20). Using the labeled data, we evaluated the following text representations and classification algorithms to select the most accurate model for NPs classification: (a) SVM using tf-idf vectors for NPs representation; (b) Bidirectional GRU using the Global Vectors for Word Representation (GloVe) model (Pennington et al., 2014) for NPs representation; (c) BERT, fine-tuned on our NPs classification task.

We applied TfidfVectorizer[7] for tf-idf text representation, utilized 200d GloVe for text representation of NPs, and implemented GRU in Keras[8]. The maximum sequence length was set to 5. We relied on the Sigmoid activation function and learned the weights using the Adam optimizer and Cross Entropy loss. We used a typical batch size of 32. We fine tuned BERT using the pre-trained English bert-base-cased model(Devlin et al., 2019), which has 12 transformer layers, 12 self-attention heads, and a hidden size of 768. We applied a pre-trained BERT

[6]https://spacy.io/

[7]https://scikit-learn.org/stable/modules/generated/sklearn.feature_extraction.text. TfidfVectorizer.html

[8]https://keras.io/

Classifier	Accuracy	HammingLoss
SVM_tf-idf	0.72	0.043
GRU_GloVe	0.76	0.049
BERT	0.89	0.022

Table 2: Results of different classifiers for NPs classification

Category	Precision	Recall	F1
Age	1.00	1.00	1.00
Date	0.92	0.92	0.92
Gender	1.00	0.67	0.80
Location	1.00	1.00	1.00
None	0.90	0.88	0.89
Symptom	0.94	0.88	0.91
Time	1.00	1.00	1.00
Micro avg	0.93	0.89	0.91
Macro avg	0.97	0.91	0.92
Weighted avg	0.93	0.89	0.91
Samples avg	0.90	0.89	0.90
Accuracy	0.89		
Hamming Loss	0.022		

Table 3: The detailed results of NPs classification using fine-tuned BERT

Symptom	#Labeled	P	R	F1
Blood Clotting	24	1.00	1.00	1.00
Brain Fog	76	0.96	1.00	0.98
Breathlessness	186	0.96	0.98	0.97
Chest Pain	45	0.95	0.95	0.95
Cough	16	1.00	1.00	1.00
Fatigue	201	0.95	1.00	0.98
Fever	45	1.00	0.80	0.89
Gastrointestinal Problems	30	1.00	1.00	1.00
Headache	32	0.77	1.00	0.87
Heart Problems	138	0.97	1.00	0.99
Joint or Muscle Pain	147	0.93	0.93	0.93
Mental Problems	69	0.92	1.00	0.96
Parosmia	18	1.00	1.00	1.00
Skin Rash	18	1.00	0.83	0.91
Sleep Disorders	24	1.00	1.00	1.00
Sore Throat	21	0.80	0.57	0.67
None	31	1.00	0.29	0.44
Macro avg		0.95	0.90	0.91
Weighted avg		0.95	0.95	0.94
Accuracy		0.95		

Table 4: The detailed results of symptom classification using fine-tuned BERT

model to produce dense vector representations for NPs, attaching a dense layer and a softmax layer to fine tune the model for our task. We used the Adam optimizer and Cross Entropy loss for training, with 1e-5 as the initial learning rate, and batch size 32.

The results of different NP classifiers are shown in Table 2. The fine-tuned BERT classifier outperformed others, so we apply it for the NPs classification. More detailed results of fine-tuned BERT are shown in Table 3.

Since we are only interested in the tweets containing Long COVID symptoms, the tweets without "Symptom" NPs were also filtered out. As a result, 61% of the data was retained for further steps.

4.3 Information Extraction from Noun Phrases

Referring to Long COVID Wikipedia[9] and other related studies (Del Rio et al., 2020; Olliaro, 2021), we summarized the long-term symptoms to 16 classes (shown in Table 4). We used semi-automatic method to label a 1K sample of symptom NPs from the 2020 dataset for training supervised classification models. First, we applied K-means with K=17, for dividing all NPs to 17 clusters (for 16 symptom classes and 1 for miscellaneous NPs describing symptoms that are not included in our list). Then, we manually corrected the clustering results, where 32.6% of each cluster instances were corrected on average. Subsequently, we used this labeled data to fine-tune BERT for a symptom NPs classification task. The labeled data was randomly split into 80% for training and 20% for test. Details of the model performance are shown in Table 4. Given this model, all of the symptom NPs were automatically labeled. We used the same configurations, as shown in 4.2 for the NPs classification, for fine tuning BERT for symptoms categorization.

For gender NPs classification, we used the zero-shot text classification pipeline[10], which is based on the Bart (Lewis et al., 2020) model pre-trained on Multi-Genre Natural Language Inference (MultiNLI) corpus[11].

We applied geopy[12] to convert the location information into geographic coordinates.

When generating word clouds for the symptom-related tweets, we calculated semantic similarity between each word and any of explored symptoms using the cosine similarity between their 300d word2vec vectors. Words with low similarity to all symptoms were discarded.

More detailed performance of information extraction is shown in Appendix A.2.

[9]https://en.wikipedia.org/wiki/Long_COVID

[10]https://discuss.huggingface.co/t/new-pipeline-for-zero-shot-text-classification/681

[11]https://cims.nyu.edu/ sbowman/multinli/

[12]https://pypi.org/project/geopy/

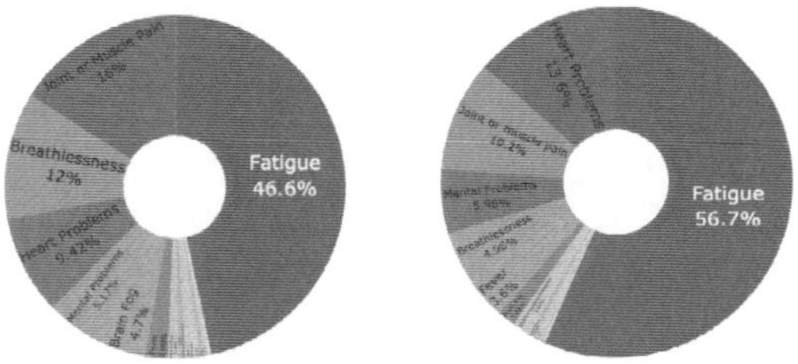

(a) May-December 2020 (b) October 2021

Figure 4: Distribution of symptoms

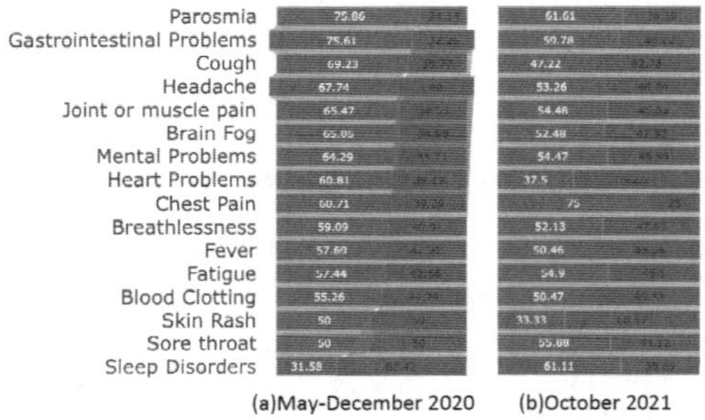

Figure 5: Gender distribution of each symptoms (Male: red; female: blue)

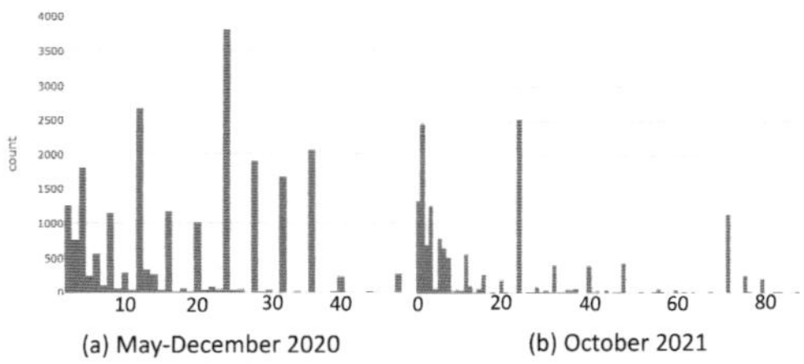

Figure 6: Duration(weeks) distribution

5 Results Analysis

After conducting information extraction with multiple pre-trained models, we performed comprehensive analysis of symptom-related data. We compared the results of May-December 2020 and the results of October 2021 to analyze the Long COVID evolution over time. The results of May-December 2020 were presented in an interactive dashboard.

Long COVID Symptoms Analysis Extracting the symptoms from the tweets, we analyzed the symptom distribution using the frequency of each symptom reported in each dataset. Fig. 4(a) shows the distribution of the symptoms in May-December 2020. From Fig. 4(a), we can see that the major symptoms are fatigue, breathlessness, joint or muscle pain, heart problems, and brain fog. Some rarely reported symptoms are headache, sleep disorders, cough, sore throat, skin rash.

Fig. 4 shows the comparison of symptom distribution in May-December 2020 and October 2021. Generally speaking, the top symptoms and rare symptoms stay approximately the same, except for the following changes. The percentages of fatigue and heart problems have increased from 46.6% to 56.7% and from 9.42% to 13.6%, respectively. The percentage of breathlessness and joint or muscle pain have decreased from 12% to 4.98% and from 16% to 10.2%, respectively. These changes may be explained by the mutations of the virus over time.

Symptoms Association with Gender We associated the extracted gender with the symptoms reported in the same tweet, analyzing the gender distribution with each symptom to explore the different experiences between men and women. Fig. 5 shows the gender distribution with symptoms of two datasets. Specifically, in our dataset of 2020, 62% of mentioned patients are reported as female, and 38% are reported as male. However, it is reported that about 30% Twitter users are female, and about 70% are male[13]. This may indicate that women are significantly more likely than men to suffer ongoing symptoms after COVID-19. Most of the symptoms appear to have an approximately equal distribution between men and women. Some very common symptoms, such as breathlessness, brain fog, and heart problems are more likely to happen to women than men. However, men are more likely to suffer from sleeping difficulties than women. And women are reported far more than men to suffer from parosmia and gastrointestinal problems.

Different from the 2020 dataset containing 62% female and 38% male, the dataset of October 2021 contains 54% female and 46% male. It still shows that women patients are more likely to be reported suffering Long COVID, however, the percentage of reported men patients is increasing. Similarly to the results of 2020, most symptoms show approximately equal distribution between men and women. The symptoms having big differences of distribution between men and women include cough and sleeping disorders.

[13]https://www.statista.com/statistics/828092/distribution-of-users-on-twitter-worldwide-gender/

Symptom	May-Dec 2020	Oct 2021
Blood Clotting	(17.898, 21.121)	(18.762, 27.016)
Brain Fog	(18.942, 20.195)	(17.156, 21.957)
Breathlessness	(17.510, 18.362)	(17.259, 20.020)
Chest Pain	(20.077, 22.510)	(8.373, 22.126)
Cough	(11.656, 14.386)	(7.177, 14.756)
Fatigue	(18.591, 19.074)	(19.788, 20.830)
Fever	(17.562, 19.207)	(14.743, 18.396)
Gastrointestinal Problems	(14.433, 16.872)	(14.858, 19.714)
Headache	(16.504, 19.029)	(10.129, 26.501)
Heart Problems	(18.692, 19.690)	(18.607, 20.303)
Joint or Muscle Pain	(18.543, 19.291)	(17.758, 20.041)
Mental Problems	(18.216, 19.515)	(22.178, 25.745)
Parosmia	(16.707, 18.956)	(15.263, 22.151)
Skin Rash	(10.241, 14.558)	(1.282, 35.117)
Sleep Disorders	(18.382, 23.617)	(10.141, 30.413)
Sore Throat	(16.472, 21.527)	(15.273, 30.998)

Table 5: The confidence intervals of symptom duration(weeks)

Symptoms Duration Associating symptoms with duration information, we analyzed for how much time people reported themselves to suffer from the Long COVID symptoms. Duration distributions of all symptoms of both datasets are shown in Fig. 6. In general, the duration of symptoms reported ranges from less than one month to more than ten months. From the comparison of symptoms duration distributions shown in Fig. 6, we can see that the distribution of October 2021 roughly follows the results of 2020. Most of the duration is less than half year, but the results of October 2021 contain a bigger proportion of duration, which is less than three months. It should be considered that some reported symptoms duration did not follow the same definition of Long COVID. However, considering the data of October 2021 observes longer time of COVID, some reported duration can reach 80 weeks.

Table. 5 shows the confidence intervals of symptoms duration in both datasets. In 2020 dataset, the duration for the most symptom categories is around five months. However, cough has been reported to last a relatively short time.

Symptoms Association with Age After extracting the age information, we linked the age and the symptom reported in the same tweet. Fig. 7 shows the distributions of age reported for 'long haulers' in our datasets and also compares the age distribution of all Twitter users[14]. The extracted age values in our datasets are mostly below 50. A possible reason is that people below 50 years old are more active on Twitter. However, despite the low percentages of age groups below 18 and above 50 among Twitter users, these age groups are reported more frequently to have Long COVID in our datasets. Notably, comparing the results of October 2021 to the results of 2020, the age group below 30 has a big proportion in the data of October 2021.

[14]https://www.statista.com/statistics/283119/age-distribution-of-global-twitter-users/

Symptom	May-Dec 2020	Oct 2021
Blood Clotting	(30.010, 36.076)	(28.692, 39.036)
Brain Fog	(35.513, 39.132)	(29.639, 35.804)
Breathlessness	(37.198, 38.987)	(31.097, 34.411)
Chest Pain	(35.191, 41.665)	(28.707, 60.403)
Cough	(16.184, 30.482)	(18.636, 46.613)
Fatigue	(35.641, 36.688)	(28.711, 29.681)
Fever	(26.829, 31.232)	(29.640, 33.714)
Gastrointestinal Problems	(38.418, 46.581)	(26.491, 32.196)
Headache	(35.162, 42.837)	(15.174, 30.825)
Heart Problems	(36.291, 38.292)	(28.497, 30.460)
Joint or Muscle Pain	(36.291, 38.292)	(30.348, 32.757)
Mental Problems	(35.916, 39.837)	(28.389, 31.763)
Parosmia	(36.460, 45.967)	(29.415, 42.908)
Sleep Disorders	(31.259, 44.740)	(8.391, 62.608)

Table 6: The age confidence intervals of each symptom

Table. 6 shows the age confidence intervals of each symptom. Comparing the results of October 2021 to the results of 2020, it can be observed that except for the increased age of cough and fever, the average age of patients experiencing other symptoms clearly decreased.

Symptoms Association with Geolocation Using the extracted geolocation information, we demonstrate geographic distributions of each symptom in the world map. As the COVID-19 pandemic has spread all over the world, the geographic distributions of May-December 2020 and October 2021 are approximately the same. Fig. 8 shows one example symptom "Joint Pain" association with geolocation based on the dataset of May-December 2020. Britain and USA have more twitter users reporting Long COVID symptoms than any other country. A possible explanation might be that people in Britain and USA are more aware about the long COVID symptoms. It can also be explained by these two countries being most popular on Twitter out of English-speaking countries[15].

Content Analysis In order to demonstrate the representative context of long COVID reports, we generated a word cloud for each month to present the most frequent symptom-related words. In gen-

[15]https://www.statista.com/statistics/242606/number-of-active-twitter-users-in-selected-countries/

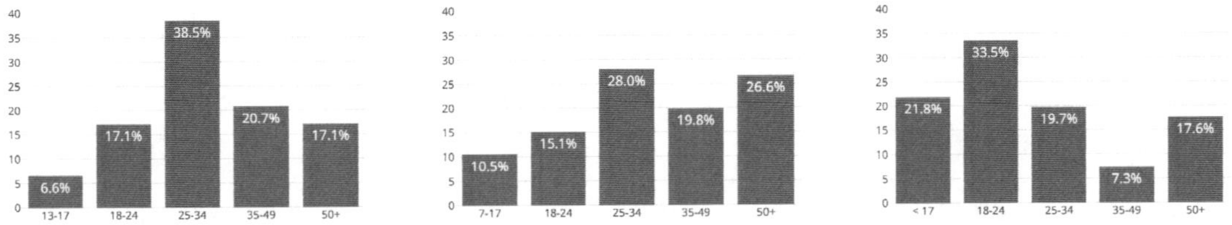

(a) Age distribution of Twitter users worldwide

(b) Age distribution in our dataset of May-December 2020

(c) Age distribution in our dataset of October 2021

Figure 7: Age distribution comparison of Twitter users and reported in our datasets

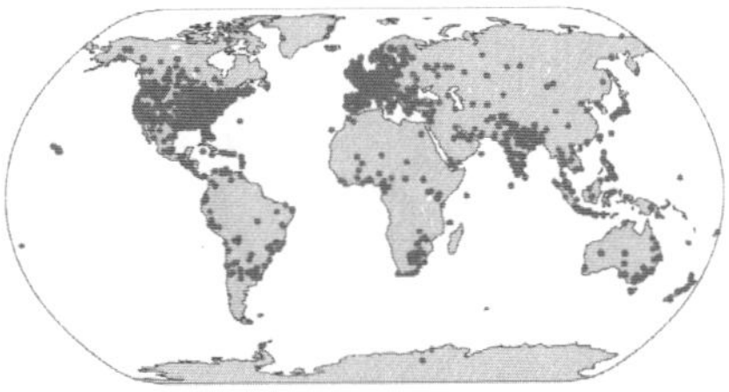

Figure 8: "Joint Pain" association with geolocation

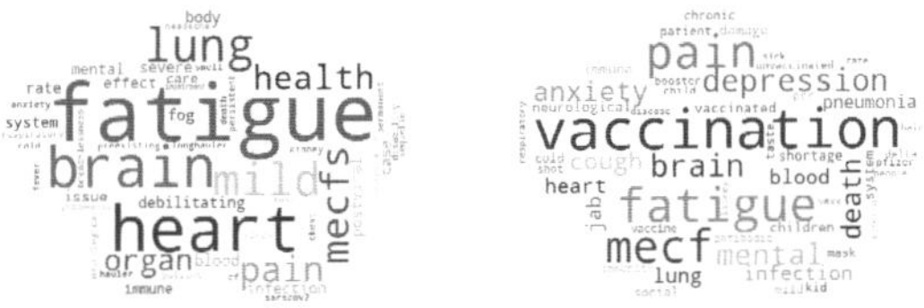

(a) October 2020

(b) October 2021

Figure 9: Word clouds

eral, the most frequent words are related to the most frequent symptoms. By presenting the word cloud on monthly basis, we explored the dynamics of the frequent words. The examples of the word clouds are shown in Fig. 9. Comparing the word clouds of October 2020 and October 2021, we can see that some common symptoms are frequently discussed in both datasets. However, considering the vaccination progress in 2021, from Fig. 9(b) we can see that vaccination-related words are frequently discussed along with Long COVID symptoms. Notably, "depression", "anxiety", and "mental", which represent the symptoms of mental problems are more frequently discussed in the dataset of 2021.

In conclusion, the results of October 2021 are partially consistent with 2020. Notably, with the evolving COVID-19 pandemic including mutations and vaccination some characteristics of Long COVID symptoms appear to be evolving over time.

6 Discussion

Some important insights can be gained from the analysis. For example, women tend to experience Long COVID more frequently than men, which is similar to the findings of some medical studies (Sudre et al., 2021; Ortona and Malorni, 2021; Bai et al., 2021; Blomberg et al., 2021). Additionally, 'mental problems' is one of the top symptoms shown in our results, which is rarely mentioned as a common symptom in other works. In our work, 'mental problems' refers to depression, anxiety, loneliness and other mental or emotional health issues. Similarly, Sarker and Ge (2021) reported 55.2% users in the Reddit dataset experiencing mental problems since their COVID onset.

7 Conclusions

In this work, we conducted a comprehensive analysis of Long COVID symptoms reported by the Twitter users with respect to their demographic and geographical characteristics. The presented case study provides detailed information and important insights about multiple aspects of long-term symptoms. The comparative analysis of two periods of time (in 2020 and 2021) shows the consistent and the evolving characteristics of the Long COVID. Furthermore, an interactive online dashboard was built to visualize the results of the 2020 dataset. Limitations of this work include the possible effect of large amounts of noise in the Twitter data on our results. Besides, the data analyzed was limited to English tweets, which might not be representative of all segments of the world population affected by COVID-19. Thus, our future work will focus on analyzing larger amounts of data in multiple languages. Symptoms co-occurrence and presence of comorbidities may also be explored in the future work. Moreover, non-binary gender class may be taken into account in the future work as well.

Ethics Justification

This work is completely based on publicly accessible Twitter data. So there is no necessity for ethical approval. As the signing of the Twitter User Agreement by the users, no further user consent is required in this work for the data to be used. The results in this paper are not fully representative because the data is only from the Twitter social media platform and only English tweets are included.

Acknowledgements

This research was partially supported by an internal grant No. 87867211 from Ben-Gurion University of the Negev Corona Task Force.

References

Francesca Bai, Daniele Tomasoni, Camilla Falcinella, Diletta Barbanotti, Roberto Castoldi, Giovanni Mulè, Matteo Augello, Debora Mondatore, Marina Allegrini, Andrea Cona, et al. 2021. Female gender is associated with "long covid" syndrome: a prospective cohort study. *Clinical Microbiology and Infection*.

Juan M Banda, Gurdas Viguruji Singh, Osaid Alser, and Daniel Prieto-Alhambra. 2020. Long-term patient-reported symptoms of covid-19: an analysis of social media data. *medRxiv*.

Bjørn Blomberg, Kristin Greve-Isdahl Mohn, Karl Albert Brokstad, Fan Zhou, Dagrun Waag Linchausen, Bent-Are Hansen, Sarah Lartey, Therese Bredholt Onyango, Kanika Kuwelker, Marianne Sævik, et al. 2021. Long covid in a prospective cohort of home-isolated patients. *Nature Medicine*, pages 1–7.

Felicity Callard and Elisa Perego. 2021. How and why patients made long covid. *Social Science & Medicine*, 268:113426.

Angelo Carfì, Roberto Bernabei, Francesco Landi, et al. 2020. Persistent symptoms in patients after acute covid-19. *Jama*, 324(6):603–605.

Emily Chen, Kristina Lerman, and Emilio Ferrara. 2020. Tracking social media discourse about the covid-19 pandemic: Development of a public coronavirus twitter data set. *JMIR Public Health and Surveillance*, 6(2):e19273.

Ricardo C Cury, Istvan Megyeri, Tony Lindsey, Robson Macedo, Juan Batlle, Shwan Kim, Brian Baker, Robert Harris, and Reese H Clark. 2021. Natural language processing and machine learning for detection of respiratory illness by chest ct imaging and tracking of covid-19 pandemic in the united states. *Radiology: Cardiothoracic Imaging*, 3(1):e200596.

Carlos Del Rio, Lauren F Collins, and Preeti Malani. 2020. Long-term health consequences of covid-19. *Jama*, 324(17):1723–1724.

J. Devlin, Ming-Wei Chang, Kenton Lee, and Kristina Toutanova. 2019. Bert: Pre-training of deep bidirectional transformers for language understanding. In *NAACL-HLT*.

Chayakrit Krittanawong, Bharat Narasimhan, Hafeez Ul Hassan Virk, Harish Narasimhan, Zhen Wang, and WH Wilson Tang. 2020. Insights from twitter about novel covid-19 symptoms. *European Heart Journal-Digital Health*, 1(1):4–5.

Naresh Kumar, Dhiraj Wasnik, Harsh Vardhan, and MK Daga. 2021. Long term health sequelae of covid-19: A review. *Journal of Advanced Research in Medicine (E-ISSN: 2349-7181 & P-ISSN: 2394-7047)*, 8(1):9–18.

Mike Lewis, Yinhan Liu, Naman Goyal, Marjan Ghazvininejad, Abdelrahman Mohamed, Omer Levy, Veselin Stoyanov, and Luke Zettlemoyer. 2020. Bart: Denoising sequence-to-sequence pre-training for natural language generation, translation, and comprehension. In *Proceedings of the 58th Annual Meeting of the Association for Computational Linguistics*, pages 7871–7880.

Raul D Mitrani, Nitika Dabas, and Jeffrey J Goldberger. 2020. Covid-19 cardiac injury: Implications for long-term surveillance and outcomes in survivors. *Heart rhythm*, 17(11):1984–1990.

Piero L Olliaro. 2021. An integrated understanding of long-term sequelae after acute covid-19. *The Lancet Respiratory Medicine*.

Elena Ortona and Walter Malorni. 2021. Long covid: to investigate immunological mechanisms and sex/gender related aspects as fundamental steps for a tailored therapy.

Jeffrey Pennington, Richard Socher, and Christopher D Manning. 2014. Glove: Global vectors for word representation. In *Proceedings of the 2014 conference on empirical methods in natural language processing (EMNLP)*, pages 1532–1543.

Abeed Sarker and Yao Ge. 2021. Mining long-covid symptoms from reddit: characterizing post-covid syndrome from patient reports. *JAMIA open*, 4(3):ooab075.

Abeed Sarker, Sahithi Lakamana, Whitney Hogg-Bremer, Angel Xie, Mohammed Ali Al-Garadi, and Yuan-Chi Yang. 2020. Self-reported covid-19 symptoms on twitter: an analysis and a research resource. *Journal of the American Medical Informatics Association*, 27(8):1310–1315.

Greg M Silverman, Himanshu S Sahoo, Nicholas E Ingraham, Monica Lupei, Michael A Puskarich, Michael Usher, James Dries, Raymond L Finzel, Eric Murray, John Sartori, et al. 2021. Nlp methods for extraction of symptoms from unstructured data for use in prognostic covid-19 analytic models. *Journal of Artificial Intelligence Research*, 72:429–474.

NPs Category	Detection Precision	Proportion
Symptom	95%	61%[1]
Patient Gender	98%	12%[2]
Patient Age	92%	5%[2]
Symptom Duration	98%	50%[2]
Patient Location	99%	23%[2]

Table A.1.1: Results of information extraction

[1] Proportion of symptom-related tweets in the dataset of May-December 2020.

[2] Proportion in symptom-related tweets.

Shubh Mohan Singh and Chaitanya Reddy. 2020. An analysis of self-reported longcovid symptoms on twitter. *medRxiv*.

Carole H Sudre, Benjamin Murray, Thomas Varsavsky, Mark S Graham, Rose S Penfold, Ruth C Bowyer, Joan Capdevila Pujol, Kerstin Klaser, Michela Antonelli, Liane S Canas, et al. 2021. Attributes and predictors of long covid. *Nature medicine*, 27(4):626–631.

Sandra Willi, Renata Lüthold, Adam Hunt, Nadescha Viviane Hänggi, Donikë Sejdiu, Camila Scaff, Nicole Bender, Kaspar Staub, and Patricia Schlagenhauf. 2021. Covid-19 sequelae in adults aged less than 50 years: a systematic review. *Travel medicine and infectious disease*, page 101995.

A Appendix

A.1 Keywords list of searching tweets

Keywords related to Long COVID are (uncased): LongCovid, Long Covid, Long haul Covid, Long hauler, Chronic Covid Syndrome (CCS), Post Covid symptoms, Long lasting symptoms, Long-term symptoms, sequelae covid, persistent symptoms.

A.2 Performance of Information Extraction

To validate the automatic labeling results, we manually verified some labeled samples. The accuracy of the validation samples is 98%. More specifically, the errors are caused by gender bias of the pre-trained model. For example, " My kid" is labeled as "male", "My mother's friend" is labeled as "female". However, the accuracy shows that the approach is valid for gender extraction.

In order to investigate the accuracy of information extraction, we manually checked some sample sets for each class label after extraction. The results are shown in Table A.1.1. Besides, because our work aims to explore the association of symptoms with gender, age, duration, and geolocation, we are interested to see the distributions of these features in symptom-related tweets. We

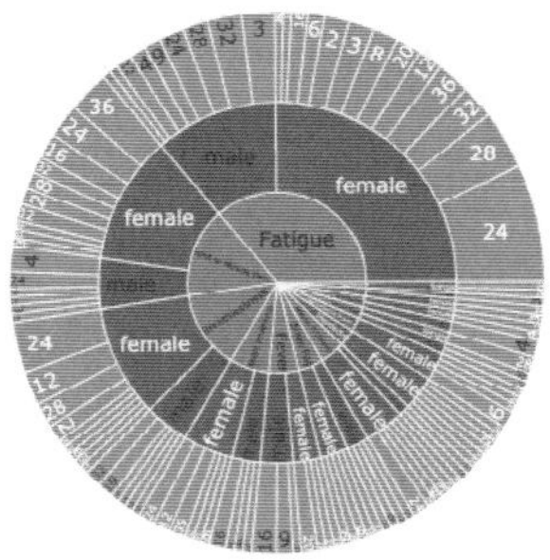

(a) Joint distribution of symptoms with gender and duration

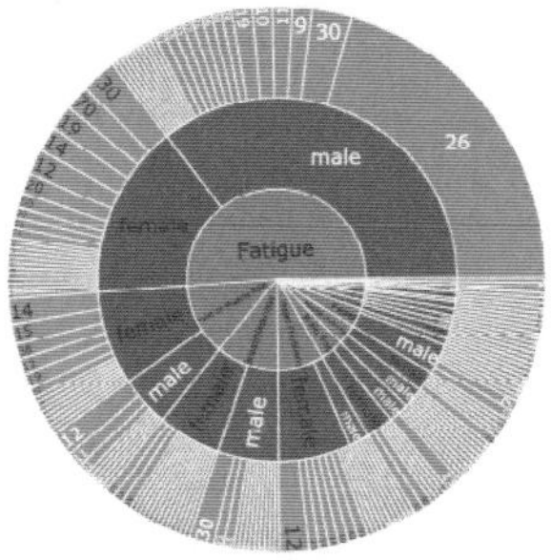

(b) Joint distribution of symptoms with gender and age

Figure A.3.1: Joint distribution in May-December 2020 Data

calculated the ratios of gender, age, duration, and location in symptom-related tweets separately. For duration extraction, NPs automatically labeled as "Time" and "Date" were utilized. About 50% of symptom-related tweets contain the relevant information, specifically 38% of them are labeled as "Time" and 12% as "Date". We summarized the key information detection accuracy and the distribution of the detected labels in Table A.1.1.

A.3 Joint Distribution

We linked symptoms with gender and duration getting the joint distribution, which demonstrates for how long time men and women were more likely to be reported experiencing certain symptoms.

We also present the joint distributions of age and gender in tweets reporting about long COVID symptoms, showing in which age group men or women were more likely to report experiencing certain symptoms. One example of the results of 2020 is shown in Fig. A.3.1, from which it can be seen that mostly women of 30 years old frequently reported to experience fatigue.

Bi-Directional Recurrent Neural Ordinary Differential Equations for Social Media Text Classification

Maunika Tamire, Srinivas Anumasa, P.K. Srijith
Computer Science and Engineering
Indian Institute of Technology Hyderabad, India
cs18mds11026@iith.ac.in, cs16resch11004@iith.ac.in, srijith@cse.iith.ac.in

Abstract

Classification of posts in social media such as Twitter is difficult due to the noisy and short nature of texts. Sequence classification models based on recurrent neural networks (RNN) are popular for classifying posts that are sequential in nature. RNNs assume the hidden representation dynamics to evolve in a discrete manner and do not consider the exact time of the posting. In this work, we propose to use recurrent neural ordinary differential equations (RNODE) for social media post classification which consider the time of posting and allow the computation of hidden representation to evolve in a time-sensitive continuous manner. In addition, we propose a novel model, Bi-directional RNODE (Bi-RNODE), which can consider the information flow in both the forward and backward directions of posting times to predict the post label. Our experiments demonstrate that RNODE and Bi-RNODE are effective for the problem of stance classification of rumours in social media.

1 Introduction

Information disseminated in social media such as Twitter can be useful for addressing several real-world problems like rumour detection, disaster management, and opinion mining. Most of these problems involve classifying social media posts into different categories based on their textual content. For example, classifying the veracity of tweets as False, True, or unverified allows one to debunk the rumours evolving in social media (Zubiaga et al., 2018a). However, social media text is extremely noisy with informal grammar, typographical errors, and irregular vocabulary. In addition, the character limit (240 characters) imposed by social media such as Twitter make it even harder to perform text classification.

Social media text classification, such as rumour stance classification[1] (Qazvinian et al., 2011; Zubiaga et al., 2016; Lukasik et al., 2019) can be addressed effectively using sequence labelling models such as long short term memory (LSTM) networks (Zubiaga et al., 2016; Augenstein et al., 2016; Kochkina et al., 2017; Zubiaga et al., 2018b,a; Dey et al., 2018; Liu et al., 2019; Tian et al., 2020). Though they consider the sequential nature of tweets, they ignore the temporal aspects associated with the tweets. The time gap between tweets varies a lot and LSTMs ignore this irregularity in tweet occurrences. They are discrete state space models where hidden representation changes from one tweet to another without considering the time difference between the tweets. Considering the exact times at which tweets occur can play an important role in determining the label. If the time gap between tweets is large, then the corresponding labels may not influence each other but can have a very high influence if they are closer.

We propose to use recurrent neural ordinary differential equations (RNODE) (Rubanova et al., 2019) and developed a novel approach bi-directional RNODE (Bi-RNODE), which can naturally consider the temporal information to perform time sensitive classification of social media posts. NODE (Chen et al., 2018) is a continuous depth deep learning model that performs transformation of feature vectors in a continuous manner using ordinary differential equation solvers. NODEs bring parameter efficiency and address model selection in deep learning to a great extent. RNODE generalizes RNN by extending NODE for time-series data by considering temporal information associated with the sequential data. Hidden representations are changed continuously by considering the temporal information.

We propose to use RNODE for the task of sequence labeling of posts, which considers arrival times of the posts for updating hidden representa-

[1] Rumour stance classification helps to identify the veracity of a rumour post by classifying the reply tweets into different stance classes such as Support, Deny, Question, Comment

Proceedings of the 2nd Workshop on Deriving Insights from User-Generated Text, pages 20 - 24
May 27, 2022 ©2022 Association for Computational Linguistics

tions and for classifying the post. In addition, we propose a novel model, Bi-RNODE, which considers not only information from the past but also from the future in predicting the label of the post. Here, continuously evolving hidden representations in the forward and backward directions in time are combined and used to predict the post label. We show the effectiveness of the proposed models on the rumour stance classification problem in Twitter using the RumourEval-2019 (Derczynski et al., 2019) dataset. We found RNODE and Bi-RNODE can improve the social media text classification by effectively making use of the temporal information and is better than LSTMs and gated recurrent units (GRU) with temporal features.

2 Background

We consider the problem of classifying social media posts into different classes. Let $\mathcal{D}$ be a collection of N posts, $\mathcal{D} = \{p_i\}_{i=1}^{N}$. Each post p_i is assumed to be a tuple containing information such as textual and contextual features $\mathbf{x}_i$, time of the post t_i and the label associated with the post y_i, thus $p_i = \{(\mathbf{x}_i, t_i, y_i)\}$. Our aim is to develop a sequence classification model which considers the temporal information t_i along with $\mathbf{x}_i$ for classifying a social media post. In particular, we consider the rumour stance classification problem in Twitter where one classifies tweets into Support, Query, Deny, and Comment class, thus $y_i \in$ Y={Support, Query, Deny, Comment}.

2.1 Neural Ordinary Differential Equations

NODE were introduced as a continuous depth alternative to Residual Networks (ResNets) (He et al., 2016). ResNets uses skip connections to avoid vanishing gradient problems when networks grow deeper. Residual block output is computed as $\mathbf{h}_{t+1} = \mathbf{h}_t + f(\mathbf{h}_t, \theta_t)$, where $f()$ is a neural network (NN) parameterized by θ_t and $\mathbf{h}_t$ representing the hidden representation at depth t. This update is similar to a step in Euler numerical technique used for solving ordinary differential equations (ODE) $\frac{d\mathbf{h}(t)}{dt} = f(\mathbf{h}(t), t, \theta)$. The sequence of residual block operations in ResNets can be seen as a solution to this ODE. Consequently, NODEs can be interpreted as a continuous equivalent of ResNets modeling the evolution of hidden representations$\mathbf{h}(t)$ over time.

For solving ODE, one can use fixed step-size numerical techniques such as Euler, Runge-Kutta or adaptive step-size methods like Dopri5(Dormand and Prince, 1980). Solving an

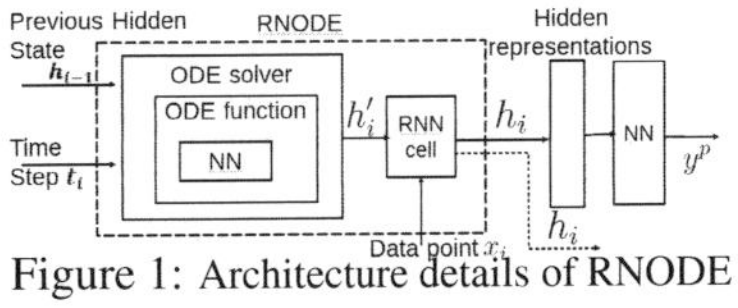

Figure 1: Architecture details of RNODE

ODE requires one to specify an initial value $\mathbf{h}(0)$ (input $\mathbf{x}$ or its transformation) and can compute the value at t using an ODE solver $ODESolverCompute(f_\theta, \mathbf{h}(0), 0, t)$. An ODE is solved until some end-time T to obtain the final hidden representation $\mathbf{h}(T)$ which is used to predict class labels $\hat{y}$. For classification problems, cross-entropy loss is used and parameters are learnt through adjoint sensitivity method (Zhuang et al., 2020; Chen et al., 2018) which provides efficient back-propagation and gradient computations.

3 Bi-Directional Recurrent NODE

LSTMs are popular for sequence classification but only considers the sequential nature of the data and ignore the temporal features associated with the data in its standard setting. As the posts occur in irregular intervals of time, the nature of a new post will be influenced by the recent posts, influence will be inversely proportional to the time gap. In these situations, it will be beneficial to use a model where the number of transformations depend on the time gap.

We propose to use RNODE which considers the arrival time and accordingly the hidden representations are transformed across time. In RNODE, the transformation of a hidden representation $\mathbf{h}(t_{i-1})$ at time t_{i-1} to $\mathbf{h}(t_i)$ at time t_i is governed by an ODE parameterized by a NN $f()$. Unlike standard LSTMs where $\mathbf{h}(t_i)$ is obtained from $\mathbf{h}(t_{i-1})$ as a single NN transformation, RNODE first obtains a hidden representation $\mathbf{h}'(t_i)$ as a solution to an ODE at time t_i with initial value $\mathbf{h}(t_{i-1})$. The number of update steps in the numerical technique used to solve this ODE depends on the time gap $t_i - t_{i-1}$ between the consecutive posts. The hidden representation $\mathbf{h}'(t_i)$ and input post $\mathbf{x}_i$ at time t_i are passed through neural network transformation (RNNCell()) to obtain final hidden representation $\mathbf{h}(t_i)$, i.e., $\mathbf{h}(t_i)$ = RNNCell($\mathbf{h}'(t_i), \mathbf{x}_i$). The process is repeated for every element $(\mathbf{x}_i, t_i)$ in the sequence. The hidden representations associated with the elements in the sequence are then passed to a neural network (NN()) to obtain the post labels. Using standard cross-entropy loss, the parameters of the models are learnt through backpropagation. Figure 1 provides the detailed architecture of the

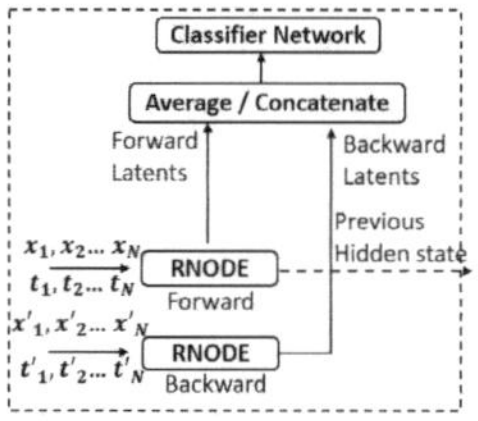

Figure 2: Bi-RNODE Architecture

RNODE model.

Bi-directional RNNs (Schuster and Paliwal, 1997) such as Bi-LSTMS (Graves et al., 2013) were proven to be successful in many sequence labeling tasks in natural language processing such as POS tagging (Huang et al., 2015). They use the information from the past and future to predict the label while standard LSTMs consider only information from the past. We propose a Bi-RNODE model, which uses the sequence of input observations from past and from the future to predict the post label at any time t. It assumes the hidden representation dynamics are influenced not only by the past posts but also by the futures posts. Unlike Bi-LSTMs, Bi-RNODE considers the exact time of the posts and their inter-arrival times in determining the transformations in the hidden representations. Bi-RNODE consists of two RNODE blocks, one performing transformations in the forward direction (in the order of posting times) and the other in the backward direction. The hidden representations H and H_b computed by forward and backward RNODE respectively are aggregated either by concatenation or by averaging appropriately to obtain a final hidden representation and is passed through a NN to obtain the post labels. Bi-RNODE is useful when a sequence of posts with their time of occurrence needs to be classified together.

Figure 2 provides an overview of Bi-RNODE model for post classification. For Bi-RNODE, an extra neural network $f_{\theta'}()$ is required to compute hidden representations $\mathbf{h}_b(t'_i)$ in the backward direction. Training in Bi-RNODE is done in a similar manner to RNODE, with cross-entropy loss and back-propagation to estimate parameters.

4 Experiments

To demonstrate the effectiveness of the proposed approaches, we consider the stance classification problem in Twitter and RumourEval-2019 (Derczynski et al., 2019) data set. This Twitter data set consists of rumours associated with eight events. Each event has a collection of tweets labelled with one of the four labels - Support, Query, Deny and Comment. We picked four major events Charliehebdo, Ferguson, Ottawashooting and Sydneysiege (each with approximately 1000 tweets per event) from RumourEval-2019 to perform experiments.

Features : For dataset preparation, each data point $\mathbf{x}_i$ associated with a Tweet includes text embedding, retweet count, favourites count, punctuation features, negative and positive word count, presence of hashtags, user mentions, URLs etc. obtained from the tweet. The text embedding of the tweet is obtained by concatenating the word embeddings [2] . Each tweet timestamp is converted to epoch time and Min-Max normalization is applied over the time stamps associated with each event to keep the duration of the event in the interval $[0, 1]$.

4.1 Experimental setup

We conducted experiments to predict the stance of social media posts propagating in *seen events* and *unseen events*.

-Seen Event Here we train, validate and test on tweets of the same event. Each event data is split 60:20:20 ratio in sequence of time. This setup helps in predicting the stance of unseen tweets of the same event.

-Unseen Event: This setup helps in evaluating performance on an *unseen event* and training on a larger dataset. Here, training and validation data are formed using data from 3 events and testing is done on the 4th event. Last 20% of the training data (after ordering based on time) are set aside for validation. During training, mini-batches are formed only from the tweets belonging to the same event.

Baselines: We compared results of our proposed RNODE and Bi-RNODE models with RNN based baselines such LSTM (Kochkina et al., 2017), Bi-LSTM (Augenstein et al., 2016), GRU (Cho et al., 2014), Bi-GRU, and Majority (labelling with most frequent class) baseline models. We also use a variant of LSTM baseline considering temporal information (Zubiaga et al., 2018b), LSTM-timeGap where the time gap of consecutive data points is included as part of the input data.

Evaluation Metrics: We consider the standard evaluation metrics such as precision, recall, F1 and in addition the AUC score to account for the data imbalance. We consider a weighted average of the

[2]Using pre-trained word2vec vectors which are trained on Google News dataset: https://code.google.com/p/word2vec, each word is represented as an embedding of size 15.

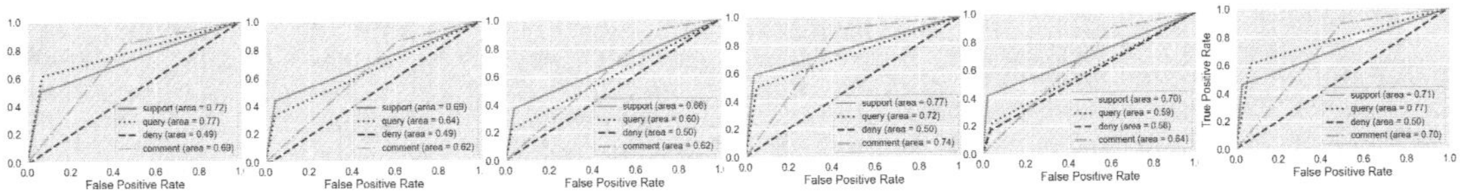

(a) RNODE (b) LSTM (c) GRU (d) Bi-RNODE (e) Bi-LSTM (f) Bi-GRU

Figure 3: ROC curves of different models trained on sydneysiege event for *seen event* experimental setup. Bi-RNODE exhibits better AUC and class separability overall classes.

Model	Charliehebdo				Ferguson				Ottawashooting			
	AUC	**F1**	**Recall**	**Precision**	**AUC**	**F1**	**Recall**	**Precision**	**AUC**	**F1**	**Recall**	**Precision**
RNODE	0.665	0.653	0.674	**0.658**	**0.600**	0.591	0.659	0.598	0.638	0.654	**0.692**	**0.670**
	0.638	0.672	0.700	**0.721**	**0.618**	0.632	0.677	**0.640**	**0.659**	**0.651**	**0.703**	0.642
Bi-RNODE	**0.696**	**0.659**	**0.693**	0.629	0.595	0.599	**0.673**	**0.641**	**0.669**	**0.667**	**0.692**	0.658
	0.651	**0.697**	**0.737**	0.690	0.615	**0.643**	**0.695**	0.635	0.652	0.624	0.662	0.618
Bi-LSTM	0.628	0.625	0.679	0.609	0.563	0.599	0.650	0.614	0.622	0.627	0.654	0.622
	0.662	0.690	0.717	0.671	0.603	0.623	0.667	0.600	0.650	0.637	0.686	0.622
Bi-GRU	0.654	0.643	0.660	0.641	0.588	0.571	0.631	0.625	0.640	0.651	0.686	0.644
	0.656	0.690	0.724	0.682	0.613	0.634	0.678	0.611	0.648	0.636	0.683	0.610
LSTM	0.625	0.600	0.637	0.637	0.567	**0.602**	0.650	0.611	0.605	0.609	0.635	0.603
	0.645	0.690	0.728	0.686	0.602	0.611	0.631	0.603	0.630	0.626	0.680	0.627
GRU	0.616	0.610	0.647	0.623	0.578	0.588	0.664	0.631	0.591	0.539	0.513	0.574
	0.682	0.695	0.713	0.686	0.614	0.640	0.687	0.623	0.638	0.632	0.683	0.618
LSTM-timeGap	0.638	0.631	0.679	0.605	0.565	0.581	0.627	0.590	0.625	0.640	0.679	0.650
	0.652	0.695	0.732	0.696	0.604	0.625	0.673	0.633	0.638	0.638	0.683	**0.651**
Majority	0.500	0.456	0.605	0.366	0.500	0.518	0.654	0.428	0.500	0.485	0.628	0.395
	0.500	0.542	0.673	0.453	0.500	0.528	0.662	0.439	0.500	0.467	0.614	0.377

Table 1: Performance of all the models on RumourEval-2019 (Derczynski et al., 2019) dataset. First and second rows of each model represents *seen event* and *unseen event* experiment results respectively.

evaluation metrics to compare the performance of models.

Hyperparameters: All the models are trained for 50 epochs with 0.01 learning rate, Adam optimizer, dropout(0.2) regularizer, batchsize of 50, hidden representation size of 64 and cross entropy as the loss function. Different hyperparameters like neural network layers (1, 2), numerical methods (Euler, RK4, Dopri5 for RNODE and Bi-RNODE) and aggregation strategy (concatenation or averaging for Bi-LSTM Bi-GRU and Bi-RNODE) are used for all the models and the best configuration is selected from the validation data for different experimental setups and train/test data splits.

4.2 Results and Analysis

The results of *seen event* and *unseen event* experiment setup can be found in Table 1, where the first and second rows for each model provides results on *seen event* and *unseen event* respectively. We can observe from Table 1 that for both *seen event* and *unseen event* experiment setup, RNODE and Bi-RNODE models performed better than the baseline models in general for all the 3 events[3]. In particular for the *seen event* setup, Bi-RNODE gives the best result outperforming RNODE and other models for most of the data sets and measures. Under *seen event* experiment on Syndneysiege event, we plot the ROC curve for all the models in Figure 3. We can observe that AUC for Figures 3(a) and 3(e) corresponding to RNODE and Bi-RNODE respectively are higher than LSTM, GRU, Bi-LSTM , and Bi-GRU.

5 Conclusion

We proposed RNODE, Bi-RNODE models for sequence classification of social media posts. These models consider temporal information of the posts and hidden representation are evolved as solution to ODE. Through experiments, we show these models perform better than LSTMs on rumour stance classification problem in Twitter

[3]Due to space constraint, Table 1 presents results for 3 events, Syndneysiege results in Figure 3.

References

Isabelle Augenstein, Tim Rocktäschel, Andreas Vlachos, and Kalina Bontcheva. 2016. Stance detection with bidirectional conditional encoding. In *Proceedings of the 2016 Conference on Empirical Methods in Natural Language Processing*, pages 876–885.

Ricky TQ Chen, Yulia Rubanova, Jesse Bettencourt, and David K Duvenaud. 2018. Neural ordinary differential equations. In *Advances in neural information processing systems*, pages 6571–6583.

Kyunghyun Cho, Bart van Merriënboer, Dzmitry Bahdanau, and Yoshua Bengio. 2014. On the properties of neural machine translation: Encoder–decoder approaches. In *Proceedings of SSST-8, Eighth Workshop on Syntax, Semantics and Structure in Statistical Translation*, pages 103–111.

Leon Derczynski, Genevieve Gorrell, Arkaitz Zubiaga, Ahmet Aker, Kalina Bontcheva, Maria Liakata, and Elena Kochkina. 2019. Rumoureval 2019 data.

Kuntal Dey, Ritvik Shrivastava, and Saroj Kaushik. 2018. Topical stance detection for twitter: A two-phase lstm model using attention. In *Advances in Information Retrieval*, pages 529–536.

John R Dormand and Peter J Prince. 1980. A family of embedded runge-kutta formulae. *Journal of computational and applied mathematics*, 6(1):19–26.

Alex Graves, Abdel-rahman Mohamed, and Geoffrey Hinton. 2013. Speech recognition with deep recurrent neural networks. In *2013 IEEE International Conference on Acoustics, Speech and Signal Processing*, pages 6645–6649.

Kaiming He, Xiangyu Zhang, Shaoqing Ren, and Jian Sun. 2016. Deep residual learning for image recognition. In *Proceedings of the IEEE conference on computer vision and pattern recognition*, pages 770–778.

Zhiheng Huang, W. Xu, and Kai Yu. 2015. Bidirectional LSTM-CRF models for sequence tagging. *ArXiv abs/1508.01991*.

Elena Kochkina, Maria Liakata, and Isabelle Augenstein. 2017. Turing at SemEval-2017 task 8: Sequential approach to rumour stance classification with branch-LSTM. In *Proceedings of the 11th International Workshop on Semantic Evaluation (SemEval-2017)*, pages 475–480.

Y. Liu, X. Jin, and H. Shen. 2019. Towards early identification of online rumors based on long short-term memory networks. *Inf. Process. Manag.*, 56:1457–1467.

Michal Lukasik, Kalina Bontcheva, Trevor Cohn, Arkaitz Zubiaga, Maria Liakata, and Rob Procter. 2019. Gaussian processes for rumour stance classification in social media. *ACM Trans. Inf. Syst.*, 37(2).

Vahed Qazvinian, Emily Rosengren, Dragomir Radev, and Qiaozhu Mei. 2011. Rumor has it: Identifying misinformation in microblogs. In *Proceedings of the 2011 Conference on Empirical Methods in Natural Language Processing*, pages 1589–1599.

Yulia Rubanova, Ricky TQ Chen, and David Duvenaud. 2019. Latent odes for irregularly-sampled time series. In *Proceedings of the 33rd International Conference on Neural Information Processing Systems*, pages 5320–5330.

Mike Schuster and Kuldip K Paliwal. 1997. Bidirectional recurrent neural networks. *IEEE transactions on Signal Processing*, 45(11):2673–2681.

Lin Tian, Xiuzhen Zhang, Yan Wang, and Huan Liu. 2020. Early detection of rumours on twitter via stance transfer learning. In *European Conference on Information Retrieval*, pages 575–588. Springer.

Juntang Zhuang, Nicha Dvornek, Xiaoxiao Li, Sekhar Tatikonda, Xenophon Papademetris, and James Duncan. 2020. Adaptive checkpoint adjoint method for gradient estimation in neural ode. In *International Conference on Machine Learning*, pages 11639–11649. PMLR.

Arkaitz Zubiaga, Ahmet Aker, Kalina Bontcheva, Maria Liakata, and Rob Procter. 2018a. Detection and resolution of rumours in social media: A survey. *ACM Computing Surveys (CSUR)*, 51(2):1–36.

Arkaitz Zubiaga, Elena Kochkina, Maria Liakata, Rob Procter, and Michal Lukasik. 2016. Stance classification in rumours as a sequential task exploiting the tree structure of social media conversations. In *Proceedings of COLING 2016, the 26th International Conference on Computational Linguistics: Technical Papers*, pages 2438–2448.

Arkaitz Zubiaga, Elena Kochkina, Maria Liakata, Rob Procter, Michal Lukasik, Kalina Bontcheva, Trevor Cohn, and Isabelle Augenstein. 2018b. Discourse-aware rumour stance classification in social media using sequential classifiers. *Information Processing & Management*, 54(2):273–290.

Author Index

Association for Computational Linguistics
209 N. Eighth Street
Stroudsburg, Pennsylvania 18360

ISBN 978-1-7138-6755-5

9 781713 867555

CURRAN ASSOCIATES INC.
proceedings.com

First Workshop on Corpus Generation and Corpus Augmentation for Machine Translation

Held at AMTA 2022

Orlando, Florida, USA
12-16 September 2022